PHANTASMIC RADIO

PHANTASMIC RADIO

ALLEN S. WEISS

Duke University Press   Durham and London   1995

© 1995 Duke University Press
All rights reserved
Printed in the United States of
America on acid-free paper ∞
Designed by Richard Eckersley
Typeset in Galliard and Pump
by Keystone Typesetting, Inc.
Library of Congress Cataloging-
in-Publication Data appear on
the last printed page of this book.

For
Lawrence Schehr, in reality;
and
Simon Carr, in surreality;
and
Toni Dove, in hyperreality.

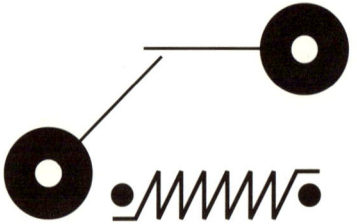

CONTENTS

ACKNOWLEDGMENTS

An earlier version of the Preface appeared as "Broken Voices, Lost Bodies: Experimental Radiophony," in Allen S. Weiss, *Perverse Desire and the Ambiguous Icon* (Albany: SUNY Press, 1994).

Chapter 1 appeared in a different form, under the title "Radio, Death, and the Devil," in Douglas Kahn and Gregory Whitehead, eds., *Wireless Imagination: Sound, Radio, and the Avant-Garde* (Cambridge; MIT Press, 1992).

Part of Chapter 2 was published as a review of John and Susan Harvith, eds., *Edison, Musicians, and the Phonograph: A Century in Retrospect* (Westport, Conn.: Greenwood Press, 1987), in *SubStance,* no. 68 (1992).

Chapter 3 is a revised version of "Mouths of Disquietude: Valère Novarina Between the Theatre of Cruelty and Écrits Bruts," in *The Drama Review,* no. 138 (1993).

Aboli bibelot d'inanité sonore. – Stéphane Mallarmé

A duck knows film is evil and that's his radio dream. – Richard Foreman

– William Carlos Williams

. . .
sometimes
there rises that
which they think in
their ignorance is a con-
fused babble of aspiring voices
not knowing what ancient
harmonies these are
to which they are
so faultily lis-
tening.

PREFACE

Radio Phantasms, Phantasmic Radio

. . . tra la la la la misère. – Antonin Artaud

In Western metaphysics, subjectivity has traditionally been conceived of as a paradox, a tension where interiority exists beneath the pressure of exteriority, and where technology develops as a metaphoric appendage of the body. The principal disjunction or aporia guiding this study is between *stream-of-consciousness* (dream logic, depth psychology, libidinal primary processes, fantasy, interiorization) and *stream-of-existence* (aleatory constructs, the concrete, montage, cut-up, structuralization). This work, polemical and passionate, is a study of transmission, circuits, disarticulation, metamorphosis, mutation — and *not* communication, closure, articulation, representation, simulacra.[1]

There is no single entity that constitutes "radio"; rather, there exists a multitude of radios. Radiophony is a heterogeneous domain, on the levels of its apparatus, its practice, its forms, and its utopias. A brief, and necessarily incomplete, sketch of some possibilities of non-mainstream concepts of radio will give an idea of this diversity. F. T. Marinetti: "wireless imagination" and futurist radio; Velimir Khlebnikov: revolutionary utopia and the fusion of mankind; Leon Trotsky: revolutionary radio; Dziga Vertoz: agit-prop and the "Radio-Eye"; Bertolt Brecht: interactive radio and public communication; Rudolf Arnheim: radiophonic specificity and the critique of visual imagination; Upton Sinclair: telepathy and mental radio; Glenn Gould: studio perfectionism and "contrapuntal radio"; William Burroughs: cut-ups and the destruction of communication; Marshall McLuhan: the primitive extension of the central nervous system; and also the labyrinthine radio narratives of Hörspiel; the diversity of community radios; free radio; guerilla radio; pirate radio; radical radio.[2]

To bring the problematic up to date, consideration of just a few radical experiments in radiophony, centered in underground Amsterdam radio, will give an idea of the broad potential of radio beyond the various stultifying "laws" that guide mainstream radio: the law of maximal inoffensiveness, the law of maximal indifference, the law of maximal financial return. A sort of perverse specialization — perhaps a manifestation of what Deleuze speaks of as a "logic of the particular" — reigns in these contemporary pirate Amsterdam radio stations, which determine the margins of aesthetic culture.[3] *Radio Romantique Urbain:* Live connections to different urban soundscapes around the world, changing cities every four hours. *Radio Privacy:* The broadcast of stolen private and intimate documents such as diaries, letters, tape-recordings, and video soundtracks. *Radio Open Ear:* Collages of different worldwide radio bands — longwave, middlewave, short- and ultrashortwave, as well as television soundtracks — from all continents. *Radio Random:* Broadcast of ten-second segments of randomly selected telephone conversations tapped from the Dutch phone network. *Radio Bug:* Investigative reporting via eavesdropping using directional microphones and bugs. *Radio Alfabet:* The reading of poems, stories, and novels from all cultures. *Radio Adventure:* Interactive listener role-playing on air, via telephone and computer linkup, partially guided by routines and scenarios suggested by the station.

Multiple (and contradictory) histories of radiophony could be constituted, depending upon both the historical paradigms chosen to guide the research and the theoretical phantasms behind the investigation. This study does not purport to be a history of experimental radio, but rather an open-ended disclosure of several crucial paradigms which could articulate such a history. Several possibilities suggest themselves, yet for our purposes three dates are emblematic: 1877, 1913, 1948.[4] If the history of mainstream radio is a suppressed field, the history of experimental radio is utterly repressed.

6 December 1877: On this date, Thomas A. Edison made the first recording of the human voice onto a tinfoil roll, singing "Mary Had a Little Lamb." As never before, voice is separated from body and eternalized in a technological mechanism — breeding the first of sundry techno-phantasies, followed by those of Villiers de l'Isle-Adam, Raymond Roussel, Alfred Jarry, etc., where the fears, hopes, and phantasms of disembodiment are finally actualized. At the very moment that the invention of the typewriter and the practice of experimental psychophysics freed words from both their gestural significance and their meaning, and at the time that psychoanalysis dissociated meaning from consciousness, phonography transformed voice into object, marking an end to several millennia of pneumatological, ontotheological belief.[5]

This is the epoch in which new metaphors of transmission and reception, as well as novel modes of the imagination, were conceived. The "animal magnetism" of mesmerism was replaced in the nineteenth century by the spiritualist manipulation of electric waves in the ether, destined to merge with the psychic waves of the departed, such that electricity would permit contact with the afterworld. By 1855 Walt Whitman had already announced "I Sing the Body Electric" as one of the poems in *Leaves of Grass;* and the entry for the year 1900 of Henry Adams's autobiography, *The Education of Henry Adams,* was entitled "The Dynamo and the Virgin." Nothing better expresses the difference between ancient and modern paradigms of aesthetics and ontology, where the rapidity and excitation of electric power would serve as the new symbol of a body now ruled by technology, without divine interference. In this century, electricity would shock us out of depression and psychosis through the use of electroshock therapy; it would fry us to death on the electric chair, that hidden modern substitute for the more theatrical guillotine; it would provide numerous prostheses for lost organs and diminished capacities.

The dynamo-virgin opposition effectively expresses the different paradigms to be established nearly a quarter of a century later at the interior of radiophonic art. The theater is a stage of history, theology, and metaphysics, of the body given to God and the Virgin, to nature and culture—the body imbued with life-force. The dynamo is something quite other, creating a new current, flow, circulation, excitation—a force closely allied with the destructive powers of technology. Electricity transformed the very form of the imagination through which we discover our utopias and dystopias, offering us Villiers de l'Isle-Adam's *The Future Eve,* Marcel Duchamp's *The Bride Stripped Bare by Her Bachelors, Even,* Karel Čapek's *R.U.R.,* the android of Fritz Lang's *Metropolis,* the erotic apparatus in Roger Vadim's *Barbarella,* as well as many other human machines, *célibataires,* and otherwise.[6] And with electricity operating in Europe today at fifty cycles—resonating at roughly G-sharp—it established a new, inexorable, unconscious tonal center which inhabits our every thought and underlies our every enunciation.

17 February 1913: This date has been inscribed as mythical in the history of modernism, marking the opening of *The International Exhibition of Modern Art,* commonly referred to as *The Armory Show.* The New York Armory Show brought modern art into public consciousness with the succès de scandale of Marcel Duchamp's *Nude Descending a Staircase,* likened by a vicious but prophetic critic to "an explosion in a shingle factory." (It is also the year Duchamp shattered musical composition with his aleatory *Musical Erratum.*) This visual explosion was echoed in the realm of sound that same year, in Luigi Russolo's futurist manifesto, *The Art of Noise.* In an epoch of increasing mechanization, and inspired by the winds of war, Russolo saw the evolution of music as progressing towards the incorporation of mechanized noise; indeed he demanded the replacement of music by noise. The limited tonal sphere of musical sound was to be broken, just as the futurist notion of the *parole in libertà* (words in freedom) freed the word from syntactic and lexical restraints. "We find far more enjoyment in the combination of the noises of trams, backfiring motors, carriages and bawling crowds than in rehearing, for example, the *Eroica* or the *Pastorale.*" Beyond Wagner's chromaticism, beyond Schoenberg's atonality, Russolo expanded the extremely limited Western musical vocabulary by including the vast variety of noises. He established the following categories of sound for a futurist orchestra: (1) rumbles, roars, explosions, crashes, splashes, booms; (2) whistles, hisses, snorts; (3) whispers, murmurs, mumbles, grumbles, gurgles; (4) screeches, creaks, rustles, buzzes, crackles, scrapes; (5) noises obtained by percussion on metal, wood, skin, stone, terracotta, and other materials; and (6) voices of animals and men: shouts, screams, groans, shrieks, howls, laughs, wheezes, sobs. These considerations were intended to change the very nature of auditory perception as well as sonic creativity. Russolo postulated that we can distinguish at least as many different noises as there are machines; as the number of machines increases, so does the quantity of discrete, perceptible noises. But, most crucially, he predicted machines built specifically to create new noises which at that moment could only be imagined — prefiguring Edgard Varèse's dream of a musical instrument with as broad a range as the musician's imagination.

But independent of these aesthetic innovations and expectations, 1913 was also the year of a momentous yet aesthetically unheralded event: the creation of the first feedback in electrical circuitry. On 31 January 1913, Edwin H. Armstrong had notarized his diagram of the first regenerative circuit, an invention which was to be the basis of radio transmission. His discovery was that the audion (vacuum tube) could be used not only as a detector of electrical waves but also, through regeneration or feedback, as a signal amplifier. Furthermore, as a generator of continuously oscillating electromagnetic waves, it could be used as a transmitter. The very first demonstration of audio amplification, by Lee de Forest in November 1913, created the "crashing sounds" of a handkerchief dropping. Radio was created — and with it, an unfortunate electronic side-effect was first heard, that of static.[7]

The confluence of these developments was of the utmost practical and symbolic import, as they provided auditory possibilities not even imagined up to that time: amplification of existing sounds, the broadcast of sound, and the creation of new sorts of noise. Though these new inventions perfectly matched the needs of the contemporary aesthetic avant-gardes, the artistic benefits were long in coming.

Audio feedback, as one example, consists of the accumulation of sound mass by establishing a continuous circuit of output and input; this is achieved by raising the sound level of the signal to such a degree that the amplified sound returns to the input, a sort of electrical or electronic solipsism. This continuous circuit feeds on itself, generating a vicious howling sound, ever increasing to a deafening shriek. The control of these effects created new musical possibilities exemplified by Jimi Hendrix's electric guitar feedback, as in his rock classic *Star Spangled Banner* solo recorded at the 1969 Woodstock festival. Yet the implications of feedback reach far beyond the strictly musical, as in the notion of a self-feeding system seeking its own catastrophe, its own sonic destruction — noise may be coaxed or pressured toward music or silence.

2 February 1948: This is the date of the non-event which inaugurates my study — the suppression of Antonin Artaud's scheduled radio broadcast of *To Have Done with the Judgment of God.* The year 1948 also marked the origin of modern radiophonic and electro-acoustic research and creativity, for it was at this moment that magnetic recording tape was perfected and began to become available for artistic purposes. The confluence of these two events — Artaud's final attempt to void his interiority, to transform psyche and suffering and body into art, *and* the technical innovation of recording tape, which henceforth permitted the experimental aesthetic simulation and disarticulation of voice as pure exteriority — established a major epistemological-aesthetic shift in the history of art.

There are indeed creative possibilities that operate at the very interior of mainstream, government, military, or commercial radio, rare as they may be: parasites and viruses that determine other limits, functions, and pleasures of radiophonic art. Yet however sophisticated the montage, most works for radio never surpass the conditions of music, theater, poetry — radio rarely realizes its truly *radiophonic* potentials. For radiophony is not only a matter of audiophonic invention, but also of sound diffusion and listener circuits or feedback. Thus the paradox of radio: a universally public transmission is heard in the most private of circumstances; the thematic specificity of each individual broadcast, its imaginary scenario, is heard within an infinitely diverse set of nonspecific situations, different for each listener; the radio's putative shared solidarity of auditors in fact achieves their atomization as well as a reification of the imagination.

René Farabet, cofounder and director of the Atelier de Création Radiophonique of Radio France, suggests that memory itself is a sort of montage structure and that the temporal present creates the ultimate sound mix.[8] At any given moment, everything we hear is "mixed" in the ear and thematically organized by the mind. All modes of such passive "montage" must be confronted, organized, and transformed by the active gesture of the *cut,* activated on all levels of radiophonic art: project, transcript, recording, cutting, cleaning, overlaying, mixing, rerecording. Here, where one may "feel the shadow of the person who worked on the piece leaning over us," montage is creative, no longer merely a "cleansing" of sound. The implications of these suggestions open phonography and radiophony far beyond the corporeal limits of the imagination. There exists a point, unlocalizable and mysterious, where listener and radio are indistinguishable. We therefore seek that realm where the voice reaches beyond its body, beyond the shadow of its corporeal origins, to become a radically original sonic object.

Hence the theme of this book, which is not primarily concerned with radio theater, *bruitage* (sound effects), *poésie sonore* (sound poetry), *musique concrète* (concrete music), or electroacoustic music. Rather, I wish to investigate the effects of what Marinetti termed the "wireless imagination" in its most extreme form. This study attempts to show how radiophony transforms the very nature of the relation between signifier and signified, and how the practice of montage established the key modernist paradigm of consciousness. This task is informed by the *motivated, nonarbitrary* relationships between signifier and signified [S/s], where the mediating term is not the slash that delineates the topography of the unconscious [/], but rather the variegated, fragile, unrepresentable flesh of the lived body. As such, this work participates in the linguistic and epistemological polemic at the center of continental philosophy — between phenomenological, structuralist, and post-structuralist hermeneutics — concerning the ontological status of body, voice, expression, and phantasms. Antonin Artaud's "body without organs" establishes the closure of the flesh after the death of God and at the opening of the nuclear age; John Cage's "imaginary landscapes" proffer the indissociability of techne and psyche; Valère Novarina reinvents the body through the word in his "theater of the ears"; Gregory Whitehead disarticulates vocal and radio circuits according to a radiophonic "principia schizophonica," whereby the radio disembody takes its place at the margins of media existence; Louis Wolfson reveals the psychotic use of the radio as a quotidian mental prophylaxis; and Christof Migone leads us

what mediates signifier and signified

to the point where solipsistic expression and universal communication become indistinguishable through perpetual and ambiguous feedback.

Between voice and wavelength, between body and electricity, the future of radio resounds.

CHAPTER I

From Schizophrenia to Schizophonica: Antonin Artaud's To Have Done with the Judgment of God

Nobody in Europe knows how to scream any more. — Antonin Artaud

What does it really mean, "To hear death in his voice?" How can one attain the impossible narrative position established from the point of view of one's own death? In 1933 Antonin Artaud gave a lecture at the Sorbonne entitled "Le Théâtre et la peste" ("The Theater and the Plague"), which was to become a chapter of his masterpiece, *Le Théâtre et son double* (*The Theater and Its Double*). His presentation is described by Anaïs Nin:

But then, imperceptibly almost, he let go of the thread we were following and began to act out dying by plague. No one quite knew when it began. To illustrate his conference, he was acting out an agony. "La Peste"

in French is so much more terrible than "The Plague" in English. But no word could describe what Artaud acted on the platform of the Sorbonne. . . . His face was contorted with anguish, one could see the perspiration dampening his hair. His eyes dilated, his muscles became cramped, his fingers struggled to retain their flexibility. He made one feel the parched and burning throat, the pains, the fever, the fire in the guts. He was in agony. He was screaming. He was delirious. He was enacting his own death, his own crucifixion.[1]

This extremely disturbing scene may serve as our prolegomenon to a consideration of a later disruption of our aesthetic field, Artaud's *Pour en finir avec le jugement de dieu* (*To Have Done with the Judgment of God*), his final work and major radiophonic creation.

Artaud's internment in psychiatric institutions – where he suffered a spiritual, symbolic, metaphysical "death," as he so often claimed – corresponded with the duration of the Second World War. Perhaps the terrible manifestations of war – the shrieks of sirens, screams, shattered and dismembered bodies, the explosions of bombs, innumerable ways to die – already evident in Artaud's theater, were displaced by Artaud once again, expressed both in his subsequent aesthetic mannerisms as well as in the more immediate and morbid symptoms of his illness. His behavior in the asylum was characterized by delusions, auditory hallucinations, repetitive ritualistic acts, coprophilia, glossolalia, and uncontrollable violent tantrums. The therapeutic response was equally violent: electroshock therapy and insulin shock therapy. (Electroshock therapy, creating violent convulsions of the body, was developed in Rome in 1938; insulin shock therapy, which puts the body in a comatose state, was developed in Vienna in 1933.) These tortures, in addition to his confinement (under extremely difficult wartime conditions), his total dispossession (all of his personal belongings, including several objects of highly symbolic value, were stolen), and his internal psychic torments, all resulted in his understanding of his situation as an *imitatio Christi,* which was at the very center of his theologically oriented paranoia.

Artaud returned to Paris in 1946 a physically broken man. (This is strikingly apparent in a comparison of photographs of Artaud taken before and during his incarceration.) Finally, his condition was mortally aggravated by a long-undiagnosed terminal rectal cancer. (When this condition was finally discovered, it was too late for treatment, and the diagnosis was withheld from Artaud, as it often was in such cases, due to the vilification and fear of cancer in that epoch. Yet given Artaud's extreme sensitivity to his body, and given the terrible pain caused by this disease, he must have known the gravity of his condition.) The manner in which cancer has been stigmatized in our century is investigated by Susan Sontag in *Illness as Metaphor*:[2] it is ill-omened, abominable, repugnant, desexualizing, corrosive, corrupting, parasitic; it is a revolt of the organs, metaphorized as demonic possession or as demonic pregnancy; cancer is, ultimately, a disease that cannot be aestheticized, and to name it is an incitement to violence. It is thus *a fortiori* a perfect disease for paranoids, where in Artaud's case it would not be too extreme an analogy to liken his cancer to the parasitic God with which he struggled during his confinement in the psychiatric institutions.

Would it be too extravagant to suggest the electric shocks that traversed and convulsed his body were countered with electric "shocks" of his own: a radiophonic transmission? The redemptive quality of such a work cannot be overlooked, nor can its role as psychic overcompensation for his previous isolation, suffering, and position as an outcast: in contrast to the demonic voices that had tormented him, he can now broadcast and thus orally universalize his passions, his art, and his cultural critique. (It would thus be a misconception to read the viciously anti-American opening passages of *To Have Done with the Judgment of God* as a political statement, especially given Artaud's antipolitical rhetoric, articulated as early as in his polemic against the Surrealists.)

In November 1947 Fernand Pouey, director of dramatic and literary broadcasts for French radio, commissioned Antonin Artaud to create a recorded work for his series *La Voix des poètes,* to be broadcast on *Radiodiffusion française.* This was the origin of Artaud's final work, *To Have Done with the Judgment of God.*[3] In May 1946 Artaud returned to Paris after nine years of incarceration in insane asylums, where during the last sixteen months at Rodez he produced the *Cahiers de Rodez* (15–21), notebooks documenting the deliria of those years, as well as the material, psychological, and spiritual conditions of his confinement. He returned a sort of tragic poet laureate, whose public celebration took place on 13 January 1947 as the famous lecture/poetry reading that he gave at the Théâtre du Vieux-Colombier, attended by many of the most notable figures of the French cultural scene, including Gide, Camus, and Breton. Here he transfixed the audience – not by reading, as planned, the poems contained in *Histoire vécue d'Artaud-Mômo,* the texts of which were interspersed with his idiosyncratic glossolalic outbursts and incantations, but by breaking down under the force of his own emotions. This period also saw the creation of *Van Gogh le suicidé de la société* (*Van Gogh, the Man Suicided by Society*), which, as we shall see, evoked Artaud's estimation of his own treatment by society and prefigured his own fate.

To Have Done with the Judgment of God was recorded in the studios of French radio between 22 and 29 November 1947, with the sound effects recorded later and added to the final tape. The broadcast was scheduled for 10:45 P.M. on Monday, 2 February 1948, and was widely announced. But at the last moment, the day before, Wladimir Porché, the director of French radio, prohibited the broadcast. Serving as the conscience of the French public, he rationalized this suppression by arguing that the French people should be spared, or indeed protected from, Artaud's scatological, vicious, and obscene anti-Catholic and anti-American pronouncements.

In immediate response, Pouey organized the selection of a sort of aesthetic jury to consider the issue. Approximately fifty artists, writers, musicians, and journalists met at the offices of *Radiodiffusion française* for a private audition of the tapes on 5 February 1948; among those present were Raymond Queneau, Roger Vitrac, Jean-Louis Barrault, Jean Cocteau, René Clair, Paul Eluard, Jean Paulhan, Maurice Nadeau, Georges Auric, Claude Mauriac, and René Char. The opinion was almost unanimously favorable; Porché nevertheless persisted in his interdiction. Pouey quit his job in protest; the tape was not broadcast, only to be given a private audition at the Théâtre Washington on the evening of 23 February 1947 (to be broadcast on French radio only a quarter century later); on 4 March 1948 Artaud died. Artaud's reaction to this crushing blow is documented in a series of letters written to Porché, Pouey, and several friends (13:121–47). In a letter to Porché, Artaud insists that it was he, Artaud, who should be revolted and scandalized by the course of events, and that even if there were violent words and frightening statements in the pieces, it was done "in an atmosphere *so far beyond life* that I do not believe that at this point there remains a public capable of being scandalized by it" (13:132). He wanted to create a "novel work which would connect with certain organic points of life, a work which causes the entire nervous system to feel illuminated as if by a miner's cap, with vibrations and consonances that invite one to corporeally emerge in order to follow, in the sky, this new, unusual and radiant Epiphany" (13:131). And in a letter to René Guilly he further insists that the greater public, those who earn their living with their blood and sweat, eagerly awaited this broadcast, unlike the dung-heap capitalists who opposed it (13:135–36). This debate was pursued publicly in the newspapers, expectedly following the general polarizations of French culture of that epoch.

[handwritten margin note: HOW DO WE KNOW OF THE "GREATER PUBLIC"?]

The description of *To Have Done with the Judgment of God* is extremely difficult, since this work exists in several different states, each highly incompatible with the others. A chronological list follows:

1. The dossier for the preparation of the broadcast (13:231nn) was compiled, in part based on an earlier project for a representation of the Last Judgment. This dossier contains many of the final elements of the work, including texts, poems, glossolalia, indications for sound effects, and so on.

2. The recordings themselves. These include readings by Artaud, Maria Casarès, Roger Blin, and Paule Thévenin, as well as sound effects provided by Artaud (drum, xylophone, and gong sounds, and a wide range of vocal effects). We should note that not all of the texts conceived as part of this work were actually edited into the tape: "Le théâtre de la cruauté" ("The Theater of Cruelty") was not recorded due to time limitations, and after the first mixing, Artaud made cuts in both the opening and concluding texts read by himself, and rerecorded the conclusion.

3. The tape was heard only in the two private auditions, and finally broadcast twenty-five years later. (See discography.)

4. The published text. A week after the first private audition, *Combat* published "Tutuguri," a part of the recorded text. In March 1948 the review *Nyza* 1 published the complete text, including those parts of the introduction and conclusion cut in the final tape. "Le Théâtre de la cruauté" was first published in the review *84* 5–6, 1948, a special issue devoted to Artaud after his death. And in April 1948, *K* published the complete text of *To Have Done with the Judgment of God* in a book that included a press dossier and a selection of letters pertinent to the events.

[handwritten margin note: CAN SUCH WORK BE TRANSLATED INTO A WRITTEN TEXT?]

Schematically, the tape is divided into the following parts: the introductory text (recited by Artaud); "Tutuguri, le rite du soleil noir" ("Tutuguri, the Rite of the Black Sun"), read by Maria Casarès; "La Recherche de la fécalité" ("The Pursuit of Fecality"), read by Roger Blin; "La Question se pose de . . ." ("The Question Arises . . . "), read by Paule Thévenin; the conclusion, read by Artaud. The recited texts are interspersed with percussive music effects, glossolalia, and screams.

The textual complexity of this work is a paradigm of why we must call into question any simply materialist or nominalist model of what constitutes an artistic text. In considering coherent themes developed within disparate texts and media, we will investigate the crucial importance of the differences – phonetic, expressive, and stylistic – between the written and the recorded texts, and in doing so we will chart the effects of the radiophonic work on the body of the artist and his auditors.

"To have done with the judgment of God" may be deemed, literally, the summation of Artaud's lifelong struggle, marking both the origins and the cataclysmic finale of his writings. This is particularly true in regard to the amphibology inherent in the phrasing of the title: it is both a question of God's judgment of Artaud and Artaud's judgment of God. In 1925, Artaud, having just joined the Surrealist movement, was appointed head of the *Bureau de Recherches Surréalistes* at which time he edited the third number of *La Révolution Surréaliste,* which bore the subtitle *1925: Fin de l'ère chrétienne* (*1925: End of the Christian Era*). Among several other short texts by Artaud, this review contained his virulent *Adresse au Pape* (*Address to the Pope*) (1**:41); in good Surrealist fashion, one might have assumed that Artaud would have circumvented the theological problem from the beginning. But as we shall see, this was far from the truth. We should also note here, however, that at the end of his life Artaud chose to begin the definitive edition of his complete works with a new version of the *Adresse au Pape,* written in October 1946.[4] This latter version begins with the diatribe

1° I renounce my baptism.

2° I shit on the christian name.

3° I jerk off on the cross of god (but masturbation, Pius XII, had never been one of my habits, and will never become one of them. Perhaps you will have to begin to understand me).

4° It is I (and not Jesus Christ) who had been crucified at Golgotha, and this occurred so that I could be held up against god and his christ, because I am a man and because god and his christ are only ideas which bear, moreover, the filthy mark of man's hand; and for me these ideas never existed. (1*:13)

wow

This revindication of his earlier polemic marks the closure of a life-long trajectory of suffering where the passions of the flesh were rarely dissociated from the spiritual passions of a theological dimension, often bearing cosmic – and markedly paranoid – proportions. To sum up the fundamental theme of these works, and of his deliria, we may cite an early entry in the *Cahiers de Rodez,* dated February 1945: "God is the monomaniac of the unconscious, the erotic of the unconscious, following the effort of conscious work" (15:315). In order to delineate this monomania, in order to understand his renunciation of God's judgment, we shall sketch out the salient features of his lifework in order to situate *To Have Done with the Judgment of God* and to consider the efficacy of his own judgment.

Ironically, or perhaps appropriately, Artaud's career began as it ended: with a rejection. In 1923 Artaud had submitted some of his poetry to *La Nouvelle Revue Française (N.R.F.),* then directed by Jacques Rivière: Rivière's rejection of these works gave rise to the now famous *Une Correspondance,* published in the *N.R.F.* 132 (1924). Rivière rejected these poems on formal grounds but found them interesting enough to wish to meet the author. In the resulting exchange of letters, Artaud outlined for the first time his theory of artistic creativity. Artaud's argument – in opposition to Rivière's insistence on the formal inadequacy of the poems – hinged on the spuriousness of the force/form distinction. Artaud claimed that the authenticity of these works was guaranteed by the suffering and passion invested in them, beyond all formal criteria. For Artaud, the formal turns of phrase characteristic of poetic language, which arise "from the profound incertitude of my thought" (1:24) are but an exteriorization of the internal passions and torments of the soul. "Thus when *I can grasp a form,* imperfect as it may be, I fix it, for fear of losing all thought" (1*:24).

[handwritten margin note: WHERE DOES AUTHORITY COME FROM? FORMAL STRUCTURE BLOCKING]

This scatteredness of my poems, these defects of form, this constant sagging of my thought, must be attributed not to a lack of practice, a lack of command of the instrument that I employed, a lack of intellectual development; but to a central collapse of the soul, a sort of erosion, both essential and fleeting, of thought, to the temporary nonpossession of the material benefits of my development, to the abnormal separation of the elements of thought (the impulse to think, at each of the terminal stratifications of thought, passing through all the states, all the bifurcations, all the localizations of thought and of form). (1:28)*

Artaud wrote so as not to go mad; he had the right to speak because he suffered. In a sophisticated use of the intentional fallacy, he explains, "I am a man whose spirit has greatly suffered, and by virtue of this I have the *right* to speak" (1*:30). This is a "right" that he was often denied. Indeed, owing to the frustrations of rejection, the torments of the soul, and the negative judgments of others, his speech was often transformed into the hyperbolic expression of pain and anger: the scream. The one poem contained in *Une Correspondance* is entitled "Cri" ("Scream" or "Cry"), where we read – in response to his current situation and in anticipation of many future impasses – of the "little celestial poet" in regard to whose work, "silence and night muzzle all impurity" (1*:31). But it was perhaps this constant struggle – with himself, his peers, his tradition, his god – that motivated him to attempt to express his deepest fears and agonies, manifested throughout his entire work. By definition, in submitting his works to the *N.R.F.,* he opened himself up to the judgment of others. This judgment was to become a determinant factor in his own self-definition, as well as the axis of his struggle against the world. "To cure me of the judgment of others, I have the entire distance that separates me from myself" (1*:27), he wrote to Rivière. But he ended the same letter with a curious formula, rather inhabitual in French: "I entrust myself to your judgment" (1*:30). Whereas he placed these early poetic works before the judgment of one man, the closure of his complete works assumes mythopoetic dimensions as this judgment is raised to a cosmic level; later, it is rather God's judgment that he must be done with, a judgment that will come to define the infinitesimally small space that delineates the self, that divides the self from itself. That space is his unconscious, haunted by God and His demons.

Artaud's role in the Surrealist movement was brief (1925–1927), central, and tragic. His appropriation of Surrealism was certainly nuanced by his already nascent poetics, more than it was influenced by Surrealist dogma. Soon after the publication of Breton's first *Manifesto of Surrealism,* Artaud (as head of the Bureau de Recherches Surréalistes) authored a memo internal to the group, known as the "Déclaration du 27 janvier 1925," which was signed by most of its members, including Breton. This text – a sort of short "Surrealist manifesto" – closes with a reiteration of Artaud's earlier position on the creative act, in distinct contradiction to Breton's more poetic model. "Surrealism is not poetic form. It is a scream of the spirit which turns back upon itself and which is desperately determined to crush its shackles, if necessary with material hammers" (1**:30). Other differences became visible: in his report, "L'Activité du bureau de recherches Surréalistes," published in *La Révolution Surréaliste* 3, Artaud explained that "Surrealism records a certain number of repulsions rather than beliefs" and ends the report by stating that "here a certain Faith is instilled; but let me be heard by coprophiliacs, aphasics, and in general by all those discredited in words and speech, the Pariahs of thought. I speak only for them" (1**:46–47). Needless to say, he was no longer speaking for the group, but against them: Artaud's desublimatory position was in marked contrast with Breton's highly refined mode of poetic sublimation. The Surrealists would not long acquiesce with this position: Artaud was denounced in *Au grand jour* (1927), where he is berated for his "veritable bestiality" and criticized because "he wanted to see in the revolution only a metamorphosis of the interior conditions of the soul, which is characteristic of the mentally defective, the impotent, and the cowardly." This terrible invective concludes: "Today we vomited out this scoundrel. We no longer see why this carrion waits any longer to convert, or, as he would no doubt say, *to declare himself Christian.*"[5] Little did they know how literally this prediction of conversion would come true, and how painfully their metaphoric reference to death would become a central trope in Artaud's own autobiographic accounts of his mental "defects."

Artaud's response, in "A la grande nuit, ou le bluff Surréaliste" ("In Darkest Night, or The Surrealist Bluff"), centered on the political interpretation of Surrealism. Artaud believed that human existence could only be changed by "a metamorphosis of the interior conditions of the soul" (1**:60), and he denied the efficacy of any possible social, material revolution. Thus the Surrealists were "revolutionaries who revolutionize nothing," mere creators of "grotesque simulacra" (1**:59–63). But Artaud himself did not escape the grotesque.

After his break with the Surrealists, Artaud devoted himself primarily to cinematic and theatrical projects, which culminated in the publication of his most influential work, *Le Théâtre et son double* (*The Theater and Its Double*) (1938). This work outlines the project for a new theatrical art that would be religious, magical, mystical, hieratic, and where theatrical events would no longer be subordinated to a written text, as was the case with Western theater up until that time. This was to be an antinaturalist, antirealist, antipsychological theater, where screams, cries, groans, and all of the dissonant sounds of the human body would bear equal importance with the spoken word, and where language itself would be utilized as a sort of incantation to create a theater of dramatic and curative magic. This desublimatory spectacle, this antitheater, is compared to the plague on the grounds that "the theater is a disease because it is the supreme equilibrium, which cannot be achieved without destruction. It invites the mind to share a delirium that exalts its energies" (4:39). The primacy of the expression of *force,* earlier made in relation to Artaud's own poetry, is now generalized for theatrical production; hence the famed notion of a "theater of cruelty," where cosmic force becomes libidinal production and where the symbolic is transformed into the corporeal rhythms of human passions and torments.

The theater is an exorcism, a summoning of energy. It is a means of channeling the passions, of making them serve something, but it must be understood not as an art or a distraction but rather as a solemn act, and this paroxysm, this solemnity, this danger must be restored to it. In order to do that it must abandon individual psychology, enter into mass passions, into the conditions of the collective spirit, grasp the collective wavelengths, in short, change the subject. (5:153; from a letter of August 1933 to Natalie Clifford Barney)

For Artaud, the double of the theater is life, where life itself is understood according to the exigencies of cruel necessity. Thus *The Theater and Its Double* proposes not only a theory of theatrical and poetic production but also a hermeneutic of Artaud's own existence. It might be said that the true "theater of cruelty" was played out in Artaud's own imaginary, on his own body, during his stay at the asylum of Rodez, where the cosmic and paranoid struggle against God's judgment was finally to take place.

In 1936 Artaud voyaged to Mexico, to visit the land of the Tarahumaras, where he became steeped in religion, myth, and magic, all of which were subsequently transposed into his own idiosyncratic and syncretic mythopoeia. This quest became the subject of the posthumously published book *Les Tarahumaras* (9), which is composed of texts written from the time of the trip up until his death, including the source of a section of *To Have Done with the Judgment of God,* "Tutuguri, le rite du soleil noir." Here, for example, he transposes part of the Indian myth and ritual into his own mythopoetic system, so that "the major tone of the Rite is precisely

THE ABOLITION OF THE CROSS" (8:79). But art proved to be quite different from ritual.

His next voyage marked the catastrophic turning point of his life, where his actual conversion to Christianity was contemporaneous with the onset of madness. His lifelong fascination with religious mysteries reached a participatory culmination when in 1937 he journeyed to Dublin carrying what he believed to be St. Patrick's (or Christ's) staff, wishing to return it to its native land. In September of that year he confessed and took communion on a Sunday morning at the Church of Jesus Christ in Dublin. Soon after, he was arrested after a fit of violence and deported to France, at which time he lost his precious cane (a terrible symbolic disaster) as well as his sanity. Thus he was to begin nine years of incarceration in French asylums, and it was only in February 1945 that he began to write continuously again, the *Cahiers de Rodez*.[6] Characteristically, the text that opens these notebooks is entitled, "Le Retour de la France aux principes sacrés" ("The Return of France to Sacred Principles") (15:9nn). But soon afterward, in a letter to Henri Parisot dated 9 September 1945, he definitively renounced his baptism and Christianity, and the stage was set for the works that he created upon his return to Paris in May 1946, especially *To Have Done with the Judgment of God*.

[margin, handwritten:] HOW COULD HE WRITE IN AN ASYLUM WHERE THOUGHT ARE MEASURE BY ALIGNMENT W/ SOCIETY → CHANCE AT FREEDOM SITUATIONAL/MATERIAL EFFECTS OF COMMUNICATION

The written project for *To Have Done with the Judgment of God* begins with a short text containing glossolalia typical of Artaud's writing at Rodez and after:

[margin:] •WWW•

kré	Everything	puc te
kré	must be arranged	puk te
pek	to a hair	li le
kre	in a fulminating	pek ti le
e	order.	kruk
pte		

Glossolalia is a type of speech or babble characteristic of certain discourses of infants, poets, schizophrenics, mediums, charismatics.[7] It is the manifestation of language at the level of its pure materiality, the realm of pure sound, where there obtains a total disjunction of signifier and signified. As such, the relation between sound and meaning breaks down through the glossolalic utterance; it is

[margin, handwritten:] 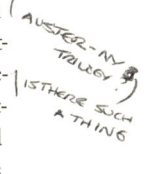 AUSTER—IN TRILOGY IS THERE SUCH A THING

[handwritten:] IF NO SIGNIFIED IS THERE COMMUNICATION?

*CAN THERE BE EXPRESSION
W/O COMMUNICATION ?*

the image of language inscribed in its excess, at the threshold of nonsense. Thus, as a pure manifestation of (expression) the meaning of glossolalia depends upon the performative, dramatic, contextual aspects of such utterances within discourse and action; meaning becomes a function of the enthusiastic expression of the body, of kinetic, gestural behavior.

In *The Theater and Its Double* Artaud already provides the rationale for the utilization of such enunciations in his theater of cruelty:

> *To make metaphysics out of a spoken language is to make language express what it usually does not express: this is to make use of it in a new, exceptional, and unaccustomed fashion; to reveal its possibilities of physical shock; to actively divide and distribute it in space; to handle intonations in an absolutely concrete manner, restoring their power to tear asunder and to really manifest something; to turn against language and its basely utilitarian, one could even say alimentary, sources, against its hunted beast origins; this is finally to consider language in its form as* Incantation. (4:56)

Updating these remarks upon his return to Paris after Rodez, he writes:

> *And shit on psalmody,*
> *bomba fulta*
> *enough seeking the true poetic psalmody,*
> *caca futra*
> *ça suffira*
> *mai danba*
> *debi davida*
> *imai davidu*
> *ebe vidu*
> *by repeating I annul*   ⁊   (23:16)

And in another text (also punctuated by glossolalia, or rather glossographia, omitted here) that may serve as an explanation of the use of glossolalia in *To Have Done with the Judgment of God,* he says: "To be rid of the idiotic and perishable stamp of baptism . . . it does not suffice to say it, but I said it and I say it again, I repeat: I renounce my baptism. And the incomprehensible words that precede this are at most imprecations against the fact of having been baptised" (22:377–78). Artaud proposes the religious, magical use of glossolalia as catharsis, as a mode of exorcism: to rid himself of God's influence and judgment.

The phonetic structures of glossolalia generally parallel those of the speaker's mother tongue (one rarely, if ever, creates a truly new language), though such enunciations are often marked by features idiosyncratic to the speaker. In Artaud's case, there is an extremely high frequency of the letter *k* in his glossolalia/glossographia, as well as of the phonetic equivalents of this sound, the hard *c, ck,* and *ch.* (We should note that the letter *k* is one of the least frequent in the French language, yet one of the most frequent consonants in Artaud's glossolalia; it is thus transformed into a highly pertinent feature of this language, and its significance must be sought.)[8]

The scatological signification of the instance of the letter/sound /k/ in Artaud's glossolalia is apparent.[9] Once again in terms of an incantatory exorcism, he writes from Rodez:

> *The expulsion of the spirits has been effected one day,*
> *not in order to protect the body, for it is spirit, but*
> *to save the soul.*
>   *cou cou la ni le ri*
>   *ca ca lo lo lo lo*
>   *cou cou roti moza*   (28:190)

And from the same period he explains that the soul is cacophony while the text is stylistics, harkening back to the distinctions established in his correspondence with Jacques Rivière. But such scatological pronouncements are far more than sheer expletives; they bear an ontological signification, which Artaud explains in a letter written from Rodez dating from same month as the previous citation: "The name of his matter is caca, and caca is the matter of the soul, which I have seen so many coffins spill out in puddles before me. The breath of bones has a center, and this center is the abyss Kah-Kah, Kah the corporeal breath of shit, which is the opium of eternal survival" (9:192).

Excrement, as a sign of death, is formless matter excluded from the organization of the symbolic order. It poses a threat to cultural formations both because it signifies a wasteful expenditure that circumvents societal modes of production and because it is an originary sign of autonomous production, of sovereign creativity bypassing societal structure of exchange. Excrement marks the body, and not the socius, as the center of production, whence comes the necessity, in the process of socializing the infant, of controlling the anal functions and establishing the anus as the place of possession and exclusion. This exclusion entails, in the major irony of human ontogenesis, the rejection of one's own body, a rejection which is the very origin of sublimation. Any desublimated return to anality in adult life marks a return of the repressed and serves as a contestation of the symbolic law.[10]

Artaud pits his own creativity against that of God, where the two are nevertheless mediated by death: "The Word is not made flesh, the flesh will be made shit and, this will henceforth be the only word of imprecation" (17:214). In restating the Johanine myth of creation, Artaud specifies the corporeal origins, the "latrines of sublimity" (12:41), the chaotic magma of existence where life and death are in constant struggle and where the soul is torn between angelic purity and diabolic filth and corruption. In a moment of hyperbolic hubris and blasphemy, Artaud proclaims that

> *When I say caca, prison, poison, penal servitude,*
> *sodomisation, assassination, urgency, thirst, a quick piss,*
> *scurvy of thirst,*
> *Sodom, Gomorrha,*
> *assassination, urgency, thirst, a quick piss,*
> *god responds inflamed logos.*   (14*:178)

Yet Artaud wishes to preclude even this response, to finally end God's judgment altogether. The diatribe becomes even more vicious, more blasphemous, in *To Have Done with the Judgment of God* where in the text of "La recherche de la fécalité" he poses the question, "Is God a being? If he is it is made of shit" (8:86). (We might note that, perhaps not coincidentally, this work was published in a journal simply entitled *K*.) Struggling against the return of the repressed, trying to resist and scorn the judgment of god and the judgment of man (which was perhaps even harsher), this final work would become a sort of epitaph, destined (in its very absence) to mark an unfulfilled possibility of radiophonic art and an unclaimed moment in the history of poetry.

•*MMW*•   All expression is informed by language *and* the body, bounded by signs *and* the libido. The figuration of force – in what might be termed the "visceral imagination" – always attempts to escape the hermeneutic circle within which force is transformed into form, into meaning. This significative evasion, beneath the threshold of sense, is precisely the level at which Artaud's texts must be read.

Given the paranoid, theological deliria specific to Artaud's condition, these corporeal/semiotic restraints must be interpreted in a very specific manner. In an early text entitled "Sur le suicide," ("On Suicide") (1925), Artaud explains,

If I kill myself, it will not be in order to destroy myself, but in order to reconstitute myself; suicide will be for me only a means of violently regaining myself, of brutally bursting into my own being, of forestalling the uncertain advances of God. By means of suicide, I reintroduce my own plan into nature, and instill for the first time the form of my volition into things. (1**:26)

Thus the force/form distinction is a matter of life and death, and the corporeal/semiotic restraint is transformed into a classic double bind, expressed on the cosmic level:

Even to be able to arrive at the point of suicide, I must await the return of my self, I need the free play of all the articulations of my being. God placed me within hopelessness as within a constellation of impasses whose radiation ended in myself. I can neither live nor die, neither not wish to die nor to live. And all men are like me. (1**:28)

The existence of God creates a double bind for Artaud: the negation at the core of the self, that which separates the self from itself, is God. As Derrida, writing on Artaud, explains, "God is thus the proper name of that which deprives us of our own nature, of our own birth; consequently he will always have spoken before us, on the sly. He is the difference which insinuates itself between myself and myself as death. This is why – such is the concept of true suicide according to Artaud – I must die away from my death in order to be reborn 'immortal' at the eye of my birth."[11] From this comes the need to kill God, to be done with his judgment, in order to gain one's own autonomy, in order to conquer the work of the negative by means of life's creative forces. The torment of my flesh, the dispossession of my self, the bewitching of my soul, the theft of my voice, all must be overcome; the task is to reduce the difference between force and form and thus transform the stigmata of God's judgment into the expression – and not the betrayal – of life. This is to be the goal of the theater of cruelty; however, an ontological pessimism reigns: "When we speak the word life, it must be understood that this does not pertain to life as we know it from its factual exterior but rather from that sort of fragile and fluctuating core untouched by forms" (4:18).

The psychological effects of this double-bind system upon Artaud are explained by Guy Rosolato: "Expulsion, for Artaud, was to be situated neither on the exterior nor in the interior of the system, as ineluctable as it might be; neither on the side of life nor on the side of death; but, through the quest for total mastery, by maintaining what became for him the impasse, the double-bind, of the simultaneous and absolute *injunctions to live and to die,* that is to say by means of the single thought incarnate in the infinite instant of passage within the circumscribed immensity of the theater: a scream."[12] The scream is the expulsion of an unbearable, impossible internal polarization between life's force and death's negation, simultaneously signifying and simulating creation and destruction. Parallel to the antithetical sense of excrement for the infant – gift or weapon – the scream, as the nonmaterial double of excrement, may be both expression and expulsion, a sign of both creation and frustration.

SCREAM

In one of the first texts written after his release from Rodez, *Suppôts et suppliciations* (*Henchmen and Suppliciations*) (1946), Artaud poses the question, "Isn't the mouth of the current human race, following the anatomical survey of the present human body, this hole of being situated just at the outlet of the hemorrhoids of Artaud's ass?" (24**:153). This conflation of humanity's mouth with Artaud's asshole is not simply a scabrous affront; this anatomical symbolism also reveals the desublimatory trajectory of Artaud's expression, of a body caught within the symbolic web and wishing to escape, of an anatomy trying to undo its own destiny. Psychoanalytic theory teaches us that speech is invested with narcissistic libido; this is true in regard to both the meaning of enunciations and the psychophysical manifestations of the speech act itself. The pleasures of speech are not merely phatic, communicative, seductive, but also autoerotic; the oral play of sensations, the very grain of the voice, creates and indicates the various pleasures and displeasures of vocal acts of expression. Spoken sounds have a primary libidinal value, for both speaker and (through identificatory introjection) auditor, before ever becoming meaningful: rhythm, harmony, euphony, even dissonance and cacophony have a passional, often erotic, quality. Ultimately, this question reaches beyond the differences between logocentrism and melocentrism, with the latter being only a trope (musication) of the former. Rather, Artaud's poetics is formed beneath the thresholds of both, in the sensate body worked through by the active libido.

CONFLATE ANUS MOUTH

SOUND HAS MEANING OUTSIDE OF "MEANING"

What Roland Barthes spoke of as the "grain of the voice" reveals the very materiality of the body within that sublimation known as speech, or song. The scream is the desublimation of speech into the body, in opposition to the sublimation of body into meaningful speech. Barthes insists that "there is no human voice in the world that is not the object of desire, or of repulsion: there is no neutral voice, and if occasionally this neuter, this whiteness of the voice appears, it is a great terror for us, as if we were to fearfully discover a frozen world, where desire is dead."[13] For Artaud, death is not heard in the voice through such a "white terror": Artaud's terror was dark, filthy, emanating from the deepest recesses of his body, a body that his discourse tried, always unsuccessfully, to rejoin.

Reducing the mouth/anus conflation to the purely physiological level, Artaud notes,

> *The honey kernel of the cyst*
> *of the lingual gum*
> *of the anal tongue*
> *of the hard palate,*
> *glottis,*
> *larynx,*
> *pharynx.* (23:328)

Here the connection is not merely symbolic: contemporary psycholinguistics teaches that the pronunciation of glottal occlusives (sounds created by closure of the glottis) creates a direct subglottal pressure on the diaphragm and the intestines, thus facilitating defecation.[14] This vortex of force is indicated by Artaud in the corporeal trajectory of gums, tongue, palate, glottis, larynx, pharynx, which explains the meaning of the apparent oxymoron of an "anal tongue" (where the translation of "langue anale" by "anal language" would be linguistically more logical but would break the physiognomic chain of expression). Thus glottal sounds are symbolic – and physiognomic – reflections of defecation: speech, as *flatus vocis,* is the ejection of a dematerialized substance, the inverse of the anal *flatus.* Such a relation is often found in psychopathological symptoms, as in the following case of a patient of Sandor Ferenczi, cited by Ivan Fónagy: "Another patient (a hysteric) suffered from two symptoms, simultaneously and with the same intensity: a glottic spasm and a spasm of the anal sphincter. If he is in a good mood, his voice is strong and flows freely and his defecation is normal, 'satisfying.' During a state of depression – especially if it is due to an insufficiency – or in his relations with his superiors, there is a simultaneously aphonia and tenesmus."[15] The glottic sphincter permits the physical and symbolic articulation of oral and anal rejection (and retention). This is primally and hyperbolically expressed by the glottal occlusive /k/, universally signified in its popular scatological form of *kaka* or *caca,* from which comes the general condemnation of the sound /k/ as ugly, filthy; this is a direct result of the corporeal displacement of anal libido directly onto such sounds.[16]

As such, these glottal vocalizations are screams of the entire body and not just the mouth. Yet these screams never fall below the threshold of meaning, since even the subglottal regions of the body are full of signification and overtly expressive. The interior of the soul speaks through the interior of the body. The realization of the intimate ties between body and language became central to Artaud's poetics:

> The least that I sought was for words to surpass the text, for the text to leave the writing, so that plain language, habitual words, and spoken syntax are forgotten; perhaps going from word to word the reader will find that I have accomplished this.
>
> I don't give a damn if my sentences sound French or Papuan, but if I drive in a violent word, I want it to suppurate in the sentence like a hundred-holed ecchymosis; a writer is not reproached for an obscene word because it is obscene, but because it is gratuitous, flat gris-gris.
>
> But who will say that it suffices for a word to sweat out its violence in the severed sentence that trails it like a severed living member; within infinity it is perhaps a fine skewer for a poet to burst forth a scream, but this is comforting only from the day that he succeeds in barding his words in such a manner that, parting from him, they would respond within the sentences of a written text as if without him, and when in rereading them he feels that these words summon him to them just as he called them to him. (23:46–47)

Rhetorically creating a "body" of the text (with its corresponding diseases and torments), Artaud wishes to recuperate a poetic or literary level to his work, beyond the raw, brutal scream. In themselves, screams might be effective to jolt us out of our commonplace literary and linguistic habits, but they in no way suffice to create a style, or a poem. Ultimately, the poetic text (including its screams) must distance itself from the poet (it must go beyond the level of sheer expression), only to return to him as an external summons. It is only in leaving the poet that the word can call out to the other and attain its own destiny.

Writing of the historical incorporation of phonetics in linguistics, Roman Jakobson cites a text that describes "a particular laryngal articulation which would, had this description been accurate, have inevitably resulted in the fatal strangulation of the speaker."[17] Yet this error is only a hyperbolic statement of the truth pertaining to the expression of anger. The state of anger or hatred considerably increases muscular tension in regard to its verbal expression. Fónagy explains, "We also observe that anger and especially hatred prolong the duration of the occlusion, and narrow the buccal canal during the articulation of frictive consonants. The evidence of glottal tomography is even clearer and more decisive. Following a hyperfunction of the sphincter muscles of the glottis, the passage of air becomes difficult. Aggressive or hateful phonation often produces a *strangled* voice. This metaphor contains the key to the explication of the gesture: one strangles oneself in order to prefigure homicide. According to a magical conception of the world, this would operate as an action that would in itself suffice to eliminate the adversary."[18] Yet on the psychophonetic level, this sort of expression is doomed to failure, since when anger erupts, the vocal cords aren't sufficiently close to vibrate, and in suppressed anger they are too tightly compressed to vibrate normally. The result of such violent muscular contractions is often a state where the vibrations of the vocal cords are "replaced by the sound of air turbulence – a *flatus vocis* – passing through the narrowed glottis."[19] To follow out, in this context, the symbolic relation between the desire to murder and the excremental expression of the *flatus vocis,* we need only consider Elias Canetti's explanation that excrement "is loaded with our whole blood guilt. By it we know what we have murdered. It is the compressed sum of all the evidence against us."[20]

An essential element of the expression of anger or hatred is the simultaneous stimulation and contraction of antagonistic muscle groups, a sort of internal battle within the body.[21] These conflicts are more than metaphoric: they express the profoundly heterogeneous functioning of what appears to be a unified, holistic body, a gestalt organization of the corporeal sensorium. Certain psychopathological conditions raise this heterogeneity, this dysfunction, to a higher and more explicit level, such as the phantasms of *disjecta membra* (the body torn apart) characteristic of schizophrenia, or the personal and cosmic apocalypses found in paranoid discourse. In a letter written from Rodez, Artaud writes of the state of sleep, where we seek ourselves "within that sort of piercing immanence, that space of unfathomable immanence where our unconscious is woven" (9:103).

The man who just lives his life never experiences himself, never really lives; like a fire that lives through the entire body in its total expanse, by dint of consuming that body, man does not live through his entire self at each moment his body, in an absolute space of the body; he is sometimes knee and sometimes foot, sometimes occiput and sometimes ear, sometimes lungs and sometimes liver, sometimes membrane and sometimes uterus, sometimes anus and sometimes nose, sometimes sex and sometimes heart, sometimes saliva and sometimes urine, sometimes aliment and sometimes sperm, sometimes excrement and sometimes idea; what I mean is that the ego or the self is not centered on a unique perception, and that the ego is not unique because it is dispersed throughout the body instead of the body being gathered around itself in an absolute sensorial equality, and composing a perception of the absolute. For man is not only dispersed in his body, he is also dispersed in the outside of things, like a corpse who forgot his own body and who swims around his body because he forgot his body and because his body forgot itself; and the man who does not live through all of himself at each instant commits the error of believing himself to be this self, mind, idea, conception, notion, which floats upon a point of the body, instead of being at every instant his entire body. (9:103–4)[22]

Once again, Artaud's perception of his own body was to serve as the basis of his theorization of the theatrical spectacle. "Even if the theater is a conflict of gestures, words, movements and noises, it is above all a conflict, a summoning of opposing forces, of clashes, resolved in time rather than space" (4:320).

Prefiguring psychoanalytic theory and Freud's claim that ego is body ego, Nietzsche already had a similar understanding of the body: "The body is a great reason, a plurality with one sense, a war and peace, a herd and a shepherd. An instrument of your body is also your little reason, my brother, which you call 'spirit' – a little instrument and toy of your great reason."[23] Yet this body, once civilized and overcivilized, bespeaks a distinct pathology, both as hypertrophied and hypotrophied:

But this is what matters least to me since I have been among men: to see that this one lacks an eye and that one an ear and a third a leg, while there are others who have lost their tongues or their noses or their heads. I see, and have seen, what is worse, and many things so vile that I do not want to speak of everything; and concerning some things I do not even like to be silent: for there are human beings who lack everything, except one thing of which they have too much – human beings who are nothing but a big eye or a big mouth or a big belly or anything at all that is big. Inverse cripples I call them.

And when I came out of my solitude and crossed over this bridge for the first time I did not trust my eyes and looked and looked again, and said at last: "An ear! An ear as big as a man!" I looked still more closely – and indeed, underneath the ear something was moving, something pitifully small and wretched and slender. And, no doubt of it, the tremendous ear was attached to a small, thin stalk – but this stalk was a human being! If one used a magnifying glass one could even recognize a tiny envious face; also, that a bloated little soul was dangling from the stalk. The people, however, told me that this great ear was not only a human being, but a great one, a genius. But I never believed the people when they spoke of great men; and I maintained my belief that it was an inverse cripple who had too little of everything and too much of one thing.[24]

We might use this passage as a parable of the effects of radiophonic art, and especially its relation to *To Have Done with the Judgment of God*.

During the early years of sound film (the 1930s), several microphones were scattered around the set to capture the sounds, and the signals were later mixed in the studio to attain a consistent, coherent, intelligible quality of speech and sound. Yet there is an inherent discrepancy between the unique viewpoint of the camera and the multifarious positioning of the microphones, such that the auditory aspect of the spectacle is fragmented and only artificially recombined. In an early article, one critic described the spectatorial position in relation to these films: "When a number of microphones are used, the resultant blend of sound may not be said to represent any given point of audition, but is the sound which would be heard by a man with five or six very long ears, said ears extending in various directions."[25] This confusion, explains Mary Ann Doane, is a confusion of media; it is caused by intermixing the radio industry and the film industry. While radio broadcasting of the epoch sought to present all sounds as coming from approximately the same spatial plane, the film industry needed to create

spatial effects through auditory means. "The presentation of all sounds as being emitted from one plane could not be sustained. For the drama played out on the Hollywood screen must be parallelled by the drama played out over the body of the spectator – a body positioned as unified and nonfragmented."[26]

This unified and nonfragmented body constitutes, of course, the "normal" perception of one's own body. The case of Artaud and *To Have Done with the Judgment of God* is radically different from that of most other radiophonic works, precisely because his relation to his body is essentially different from that of most other radiophonic artists and most other spectators. For Artaud, the shattered, disoriented, delirious, ecstatic body was the norm; the unified body was what he fought, what he saw as being at the base of an insipid Western theatricality based on narrative, psychological drama. Ironically, the failure of sound in those early films indicates what could have been utilized as a structural, technical formula for a successful radiophonic presentation of the theater of cruelty. This was not, however, the case. To a certain extent, *To Have Done with the Judgment of God* failed due to the structural features of recording: Artaud's screams – initially bloodcurdling despite the theoretically low coefficient of success of the expression of anger – lose their effect upon repeated auditions (one of the dubious benefits of the recorded arts resulting in the retrospective transformation of spontaneity into banality through repetition)[27] and their strength upon regulation of the level of amplitude; his blasphemies, injunctions, and vituperations become texts for the archives; his shattered body becomes whole and normal through the effects of monaural recording; and transmission of his work becomes, finally, not the summit of the theater of cruelty but rather a "primitive" example of the radiophonic arts.

But perhaps this failure was exemplary and characteristic of Artaud's lifework. In response to a survey on suicide published in *La Révolution Surréaliste,* no. 3, Artaud speaks of the hypothetical, incomprehensible, unrepresentable nature of this act. And yet, he writes,

I suffer frightfully from life. There is no state that I can reach. And most certainly I am long dead, I am already suicided. That is to say, I have already been suicided. But what would you think of an anterior suicide, of a suicide that would make us retrace our steps, but from the other side of existence, and not from the side of death. (1**:21–22)

Artaud was already suicided at the very beginning of his existence, and *To Have Done with the Judgment of God* was the completion of this suicide by society, just as Artaud explained that Van Gogh was "the man suicided by society." The recording stole his voice; the radio dissimulated his body; the bureaucracy suppressed the broadcast; and a month later, on 4 March 1948, Artaud died – of rectal cancer. His scatological pronouncements, his accentuation of the phoneme /k/ in his glossolalia, his extreme glottal occlusives – which permitted a violent vocalization of the passions and an even more violent, but secret, anal *flatus vocis* – were all matters of life and death. Artaud was the man suicided by society.

Though *To Have Done with the Judgment of God* does indeed participate in that creative delirium of which Artaud speaks, often revealing the chaotic, terrifying underside of human life, it is hardly an example of the *Gesamtkunstwerk,* the total artwork incorporating and expanding all the artistic media that he intended the theater of cruelty to be. Here, he was simultaneously torn between the contradictory demands of his own poetics *and* the conflicts between the structural features of radio and recording and the necessities of the theater. He provides the rationale for this broadcast in terms of "THE OBLIGATION of the writer, the poet, not to cowardly close himself up in text, a book, a review from which he will never again depart, but to the contrary to go outside, to shake up, to attack the public spirit, otherwise what's the use?" (13:136–37). He had already understood that for a writer the book is a tomb, and he leaves a great part of the creative act to his readers; he explains of his glossolalia that they can only be read, scanned, stressed, rhythmically, and that each reader must discover his own reading (9:188–89). The writer and readers must go beyond the dead letter of the text and bring the word to life. But is the radio any less a tomb? Is it not in a sense the tomb of the book, creating another sort of "dead letter" that vibrates? But this leads to the paradox of all representation, the internal contradiction of all spectacle: the more complete the spectacle, the less is left for the imagination; the more that is left for the imagination, the more impoverished the spectacle. Furthermore, because of the very nature of expression itself — the inadequacies of which Artaud had already charted in his letters to Jacques Rivière and continued to expound upon throughout his entire career – all representation can be but a mere shadow of the conditions of the interior life, the passions and torments of the soul.

In recording, the organic rhythms of the human voice are hypostatized and ultimately destroyed by mechanical reproduction, and then ironically these lost body rhythms are returned by electromechanical means. Thus recording produces an exteriorization and transformation of the voice, a sort of dispossession of the self. Recording and radio – through a sort of sympathetic magic – entail a theft of the voice and a disappearance of the body, a radical accentuation of the mind/body split, with its concomitant anguish. Whence came the terrible, tragic irony of Artaud's creation of this recorded radiophonic piece: *To Have Done with the Judgment of God* reduplicated, in the artwork, the very structure of the theological and psychopathological conditions that he fought so long to overcome.

Recording the voice poses an ontological risk: the recorded voice is the stolen voice that returns to the self as the hallucinatory presence of the voice of another. This other's voice may be the voice of God, as is often the case in paranoid experiences, and as was the case for Artaud during the period of his madness. In paranoid projections, one's own voice is hallucinated as coming from without, as a divine or diabolic presence speaking the forbidden thoughts of unspeakable desires or unbearable prohibitions. The quotidian, empirical aspects of such an exteriorization of sound without image are outlined by Pierre Schaeffer, and discussed by Michel Chion, in terms of the notion of an *acousmetre*.[28] Radio is, *a fortiori*, the acousmetric medium, where the sound always appears without a corresponding image. This concrete presence and generality of the pure materiality of sounds by themselves bears all of the features traditionally attributed to the Judeo-Christian God and proffers the oftentimes paranoid invitation for us to lose ourselves in its totality. These features of the disincarnate voice – ubiquity, panopticism, omniscience, omnipotence – cause the radiophonic work to return as hallucination and phantasm; it is thus not unusual to find the radio fantasized as receiving messages from the beyond, serving as a spiritual transmitter in overcompensation for a psychotic dissociation from one's own body. With no visible body emitting the sound, and with no image whatsoever to anchor the sound, the radiophonic work leaves a sufficient space for fantasizing, a space large enough to contain the megalomaniacal projections of the most severe paranoia, the theological projections of the most extreme mysticism with the concomitant projections of the grandest God. Thus in terms of *To Have Done with the Judgment of God,* we must ask whether this work achieved the successful ex-orcism of God, so that it was the voices of Artaud's muse that we heard, or whether this work ironically presented yet one more stage of his paranoid struggle against God, yet one more instance of the voice of divine judgment.

Psychoanalytic theory teaches that figures of style and modes of expression are remotivated and reformalized in order to serve as ego-defense mechanisms, especially in the case of schizophrenia. Thus figurative uses may be taken literally, or literal statements may be rhetorically transformed, as verbal signs of unconscious thought processes. The very problem of style as formalization or demotivation must be considered in its function as a mechanism of defense, in direct relation to libidinal, corporeal operation.[29] What does it mean that Artaud, in the final mix for the broadcast of *To Have Done with the Judgment of God* suppressed the glossolalia and sentence ("Everything must be arranged to a hair in a fulminat-ing order") with which the work was to have begun according to the written project? And that he didn't replace it with either the screams or the bruitage with which he would punctuate the later articulations of the texts but rather began with a drumroll, fol-lowed immediately by the diatribe of the introductory text? Why were his screams of "rage" (hardly stifled) in fact highly theatrical and neither particularly incantatory nor shocking but rather some-what poetic? Artaud certainly wished to create a broadcast that would break with conventions. But if to a certain extent recording and broadcast technologies conventionalize performance – by fix-ing it for endless repetition, and by flattening it out to exclude extreme effects undesirable for the exigencies of the apparatus and the aesthetics of the recording and broadcast bureaucracies – then the paradox of Artaud's attempt is evident. This is its ultimate failure: an antirepresentational representation; a spontaneous fix-ing; a nonbroadcast; an affront against the public "spirit," which was also a disfiguration of Artaud's own work. The return of the repressed was transfigured according to the exigencies of the radio-phonic art, where Artaud's voice was severed from his body, made an autonomous object in the world, and cast off to pursue its own destiny.

Artaud's expectations about the aesthetic possibilities of radio-phonic transmission were betrayed both by the suppression of the broadcast *and* by the radiophonic specificity of this new art form. The sheer numerical and geographical advantages of radio over theater were offset by the loss of visual presence and the terrible potential of unchanging repetition. "Cruelty" is thus to be redefined and redirected – but it always returns to haunt and define Artaud. His final work offered no escape. The fate of this work, *To Have Done with the Judgment of God,* is now an integral part of the history of modernist art and philosophy.[30] Perhaps it can finally be approximately heard.

CHAPTER 2

The Radio as Musical Instrument: John Cage's Imaginary landscapes

Euphonic, aphonic. – Antonin Artaud

Recording is always more than representation, bearing the stamp of both the technical aspects of the apparatus and the stylistic demands of the technician. We know that Thomas Edison, in great part because of his deafness, could not stand complex musical textures or pungent harmonies; he found tremolo to be a distinct defect of the human voice, and believed that a voice without vibrato was preferable, since it emerged more clearly on a recording; he preferred low tones to high ones; he despised extreme dynamics; he disliked the violin because it hurt his ears, and especially abhorred octaves played on this instrument; he thought that chromatic runs distracted from the melodic line; and even wanted to know whether a tune could be written solely with thirds and sixths; and, in his scientific perfectionism, he detested "extraneous" noises, such as the squeaking of flute keys, the thumping of piano felts, the turning of pages, gutteral vocal sounds – and even breathing! In short, he was not exactly a lover of serious music. The result:

Edison considered dramatic personality intrusive on discs and developed a stringent, mechanical perfection aesthetic for recordings that included purity of tone, extreme clarity of enunciation, and the abolition of extraneous noises, which, he conceded, would not be objectionable in the concert hall.[1]

Today – when extreme reproductive fidelity and clarity have been made possible by digital tape recording and laser playback technology – we find a double irony in such an antimusical perfectionism. First, by eliminating the noises inherent in earlier electronic recording and playback systems (tape hiss, microphonic distortion, vinyl pops and scratches, etc.), digital and laser systems permit the perception of "extraneous" noises of the music itself, noises previously covered over by electronic and ambient sounds: a bit too much rosin on bows, slightly too heavy breathing, the rustling of feet or clothes, and so forth. In Edison's time, it was the imperfection of recording technology that produced unwanted noises; now it is the very perfection of the system that does so. The second irony is that recorded music has indeed approached perfection since the advent of tape in 1948 – but at a price. Practically no recording is really "live," as few musicians or conductors would let pass on record a flawed performance. They all make mistakes; yet, quite simply, few release them! Thus splices are almost invariably a feature of recorded music: studio sessions include remakes (of entire pieces or entire passages, of certain sections or single notes – whatever is needed to correct an error); "live" concert recordings often consist of several concerts spliced together, with additional postconcert work recorded and spliced in or overdubbed when necessary.

Edison, in a moment of technical hubris, claimed: "I am like a phonograph."[2] Similarly, the narrator of Thomas Bernhard's novel *Der Untergeher* [The Loser] (1983) – abandoning his musical career in despair before the perfection of his fellow Mozarteum student Glenn Gould – informs us that Gould actually wanted to *be-*

come the piano. What is in question is musical perfection. But of course, perfectionism is idealization, and the onset of recording created an irrevocable split in what constitutes the perfect musical rendition between the different exigencies and possibilities of concertizing and studio recording. *Concert expression* entails inevitable technical flaws (bad acoustics, where certain musical sounds get totally lost in certain spots of concert halls such as the Philharmonic in New York; the inevitable body sounds of the musicians; distracting ambient sounds inevitable in any human gathering; etc.) as well as strictly musical mistakes (missed notes and so forth). *Studio perfectionism* most often entails a loss of spontaneity, idiosyncrasy, and expression, due to the desire for technical perfection, clarity of sound, distinct instrumental balances, and musical note-perfect performance.

In our age of musical reproducibility, "recording is an *a fortiori* idealized version of an artist's output at one particular period of his life," explains the cellist Janos Starker.[3] The recorded performance should be seen not as the definitive performance, but merely as a particular one – and furthermore one that is usually artificially tampered with. But the problem is that the "perfectibility" of recording procedures and the repeatability of listening possibilities surround recordings with an aura of definitive value. The question of realism, "concert realism," is central to the problem of recording: is the recording and mixing supposed to approximate a concert situation, *or* the intentions of the composer, *or* the perfection made possible by the taping situation, *or* must it be modified in overcompensation for the (statistically varying and relatively poor) quality of home playback equipment in less-than-ideal surroundings?

The possibilities of recording and post-recording manipulation are manifold. The use of highlighting – making a recorded instrument dynamically stand out from the rest of the orchestra – is a case in point. This can be accomplished either by the specific use of microphones to change balancing during recording, or by post-recording balancing achieved during the mixing of the different tracks. The rationale for such effects is to compensate for the visual cues that in part determine the balance between instruments in concert situations, and which are obviously lost in recording. Yet nearly surreal cases obtain in extreme examples of these effects, such as the following, pointed out by Gunther Schuller. In Stokowski's version of Khachaturian's *Second Symphony* (UA U-8002), a single flute, by means of highlighting, is made to sound as loud as the entire brass section at the climax of one movement![4] Nikolaus Harnoncourt provides a typical example of another choice that must often be made:

In Mozart's symphonies, for instance, you hear a lot of arpeggios which give a melting chordal sound in the proper hall. A recording engineer would not accept that. He would like to hear the arpeggio as it is written in the score. And the listener who becomes accustomed to this kind of listening will hear not the music but the skeleton of the music, because the music is formed after being melted in the hall.[5]

Which "realism" is to be chosen: that of the score *or* of the performance *or* of the recording? The diverse "realist" aims of recording thus determine the mode of idealism manifested by any given work. Indeed, the often exaggerated desire for performative "authenticity," combined with the mimetic quest for perfection in recording – often leading to the dullest music – is a reaction against a "Romanticism" which entails extreme manifestations of interpretation and expression in performance.

Due to the necessity of instrumental clarity and note-perfect technical mastery in recording, splicing is inevitable. What might have been understood by some as Glenn Gould's anomalous, eccentric position of having become a uniquely "recording" artist – striving for perfection through the art of splicing – is in fact what nearly *every* recording artist *necessarily* does during both studio and especially live recording. With the practice of sound recording and editing, we discover the technodream of musical perfectibility, epitomized by the career of Gould. Gould's legendary text, "The Prospects of Recording" (1966), outlines both the effects of recording on musical composition *and* the utopian limits of musical possibility established by electronic sound reproduction. The influence of recording paradigms on modern musical *composition* includes:

the reiterated note pattern, with measured crescendo and diminuendo; the dynamic comparison between close-up and far-distant statements of the same configuration; the quasimechanical ritard or accelerando; above all, the possibility of a controlled release and attack of sound.[6]

But recording has also changed the very patterns and expectations of musical *listening*. Musical performance is now associated with a new extreme of "analytic clarity, immediacy, and indeed almost tactile proximity" (certainly in part a compensatory mechanism for the total loss of visual perception in the sound recording process); microphonic sensitivity – what Gould refers to as the possibility of "microphonic dissection" – has created both instrumental balances and sound discriminations unavailable in live symphonic spaces; listener control of sophisticated, ultrasensitive home stereophonic equipment permits subtle gradations within an infinite set of different playback "performances" (thus establishing the listener as a composer after-the-fact, complicating the entire question of authorship, where the composer, like the sound, becomes a function of mixing); and an ideal or utopian performance becomes possible by splicing together different musical entities in order to create an optimum effect. An example of the latter offered by Gould is of a high C sung by Elisabeth Schwarzkopf that is appended to Kirsten Flagstad's part in a recording of *Tristan*. (Gould demonstrated in several experiments that it is nearly impossible to locate a properly made splice by listening for an error; it can more likely be found by listening for a too-perfect articulation in a difficult passage.)

In fact, we can even recompose entire symphonies utilizing this recombinatory technique, as in Gould's example of the possibility of editing together Bruno Walter's performance of the exposition and recapitulation of the first movement of Beethoven's *Fifth Symphony* with Klemperer's handling of the developmental section. Gould: "Because of this complexity, because so many different levels of participation will, in fact, be merged in the final result, the individualized information concepts which define the nature of identity and authorship will become very much less imposing."[7] Of course, the practice of musical transcription had already complicated questions of authorship, creating hybrid entities exemplified by such works as Franz Liszt's piano transcriptions of Schubert *lieder;* Ferruccio Busoni's piano transcriptions of Bach, culminating in his *Fantasia Contrappuntistica;* or Gould's own transcription of Wagner's *Siegfried Idyll* for solo piano. Thus Gould concludes – in a very different vein from Artaud or Cage – that "the audience would be the artist and their life would be art."[8]

Gould's practice is idiosyncratic to the extreme, and proposes a limit-case of recording possibilities. Nevertheless, the ironic result is that recording sets an audible standard of musical perfection (i.e., not missing a single note, not making a single error) that simply cannot be met in concert situations. In turn, many concertizers try to imitate the recorded sound.

And some conductors, such as Solti, train their orchestras to imitate recorded sound – the Chicago Symphony has developed an incredibly loud, brilliant sound, a clarity of detail, and a perfection of performance, all qualities that are derived from recordings.[9]

But the influence of recording is not always so salutary, since many young musicians and conductors prepare for concertizing by listening to and imitating recordings, rather than by reading the score, a practice which mitigates against individual expression and produces mannerist playing, a fact lamented by viola player Michael Tree of the Guarneri Quartet. On the same topic, violinist Miha Pogacnik, speaking of one of his students who would prepare in this manner, further notes: "But this was reflected in his playing: two measures of poor Milstein here, four measures of second-rate Oistrakh and Szeryng there. You could notice imitation of the types of details that recording transmits."[10] Pogacnik, in refusing to record, espouses a myth opposed to that of Gould, stressing the Romantic notion of directly communicable musical emotivity, style, and passion.

Finally, how does the listener, or indeed the performer, choose between the two? To say that recorded music does not simply reproduce live music, but is another distinct art form, or to say that the recorded work is but one (retouched) performance among many others (live and recorded) of any given work, only begs the question. A choice, or at least a differentiation, must be made. Recording engineers and producers have been deemed both artists and meddlers, in consideration of their ultimate powers over the final recorded musical product. In *The Recording Angel,* Evan Eisenberg explains what is at stake in musical recording, detailing the three major paradigms: (1) take a "sound photograph," that is, merely attempting to reproduce a given performance; (2) extract "an impossibly perfect performance"; (3) create an entirely new entity (as did Gould).[11] How must we finally judge these issues?

Further paradoxes obtain regarding the recording of non-Western vocal music. The late avant-garde filmmaker and musicologist Harry Smith explains:

a lot of experiences are lumped together as songs which probably aren't. Like tonal languages, as in Uruba, lots of things that were identified as songs turned out to be poetry that is recited at a certain pitch. Or a Seneca thing which is spoken but because it's transcribed from a tape recorder, it is possible to indicate what tone each word is sounded on. Because of this possibility of transcription from tape recordings it becomes very difficult to determine where speech ended and singing began. It is an artifact of the technical methods of handling the productions of peoples' vocal chords that classifies certain things as songs.[12]

Not only does this complicate ethnological and aesthetic issues of the classification of non-Western music, but these complications in turn establish new musical forms and musicological considerations within the context of Western music, imbued as it presently is with its worldwide counterparts. Thus, as Gould suggests, even if the possibilities of sound recording establish the archival aural equivalent of Malraux's "museum without walls," we nevertheless need new modes of categorization and judgment regarding the contents of such archives. Not only do qualitative judgments change, but there must also be a shift in the entire consideration of what enters the musical domain and how that domain is to be defined and transformed.

Recent theoretical work on audio and radio art has proposed hyperbolic possibilities of recording technology, going far beyond music: Douglas Kahn has analyzed the realm of virtual sound realities, which will guide the creation of future electronic recording equipment according to as-of-yet unimagined compositional desires – far beyond contemporary synthesizers and digital sampling devices – more pitched to active performance than passive recording, and based upon paradigms *not* limited by "the weight of music." As such, "composition and performance will have incredible transformative capacity over all elements of the sensorium, including the actual venue and the corporeality of everyone "present."[13] It is the origins of such techniques, expectations, and phantasms to which we shall now turn.

Upon leaving the studio after the session where the sound effects for *To Have Done with the Judgment of God* were recorded, Artaud declared, laughing, "Well, until now I was only a writer, actor, director, sketcher; now I'm a musician" (8:358). Indeed, the percussive, xylophonic, glossolalic, and guttural sounds that he created for this work constituted music, a sort of *musique brute* or *musique pauvre,* entirely in the spirit of Artaud's theater of cruelty. His screams became poetry and his noises became music, in an attempt to express the inexpressible, profound, chaotic essence of human existence, of cruel reality, where art becomes life.

Listening to this new sort of music imbued with noise presents the greatest difficulty in relation to the classic structures of Western music. Consider, for example, the fact that an audio engineer wishing to determine the acoustic structure of a sound of a given duration must take 40 times more measures for a noise than for a spoken vowel, and 250 times more measures for noise than for a sung one.[14] Thus the complexity of noise – a nearly random sound structure – is inexorably more difficult to listen to and grasp in its intricacies than that of song. The quasi-hypnotic effect expected of musical regularity (rhythmic, melodic, and harmonic) is shattered by the shock effects of Artaud's musical *bruitage*. This follows from his conception of the extreme effects of sound in the theater, expressed in an early manifesto, *Le théâtre Alfred Jarry* (1926): "The spectator who comes to us knows that he has just exposed himself to a true operation, where not only his mind but also his senses and his flesh are at stake. He will henceforth go to the theater as he goes to the surgeon or the dentist" (2:22).

Artaud's earliest musical project was the libretto he wrote for Edgard Varèse's prospective (but never written) opera, *L'Astronome*.[15] Artaud's work, entitled *Il n'y a plus de firmament* (*There is No Longer Any Firmament*, circa 1932), opens in a manner such that his proposed sound effects would prelude, merge with, or probably even overpower Varèse's music. The first movement begins:

Darkness. Explosions in this darkness. Harmonies suddenly broken off. Harsh sounds. Depressurized soundings.

The music will give the impression of a distant cataclysm and will fill the room, falling as from vertiginous heights. Chords will originate in the sky and then deteriorate, going from one extreme to the other. Sounds will fall as if from very high, then suddenly stop and spread out in bursts, forming vaults and parasols. Tiers of sounds. . . .

The sounds and light will surge out in fits and starts with jolts of a magnified Morse code telegraph, but this will be to Morse code what the music of the spheres heard by Bach is to Massenet's Clair de lune. (2:107)

Furthermore, in an archetypically Artaudian figure we find the human body itself transformed into a musical instrument in the third movement:

Then the noise of a bizarre drum envelops everything, a nearly human noise which begins sharply and ends dully, always the same noise; and then we see enter a woman with an enormous belly, upon which two men alternately strike with drumbeats. (2:118)

During the same period, in an interview regarding his play *Les Cenci* (1935), Artaud explains the staging, which would include the use of the Ondes Martenot (an early electric musical instrument), recordings of the huge bells of the cathedral of Nôtre-Dame of Paris, and most shockingly, recordings of factory machine noises, "which would have their place in torture chambers of the Middle Ages" (5:219).

The year in which Artaud produced *To Have Done with the Judgment of God,* 1948, was a pivotal year in the history of twentieth-century music.[16] It was the year in which Olivier Messiaen completed his great *Turangalîla-Symphonie,* with its extravagant percussive effects and extended percussion sections, extreme dynamic range (he was one of the first composers to write extended moments of silence into his works), "sheets of sound" produced by complex sustained chords, use of the Ondes Martenot (Messiaen pioneered the use of this instrument, and this symphony provides its major presence as a lead instrument), sacred inspiration, trance effects, and exotic influences (Hindu and ancient Greek scales, Balinese sonorities, Gregorian plainchant aspects, etc.). The parallels with Artaud's project are striking, and one may imagine that certain of Messiaen's works (notably the *Turangalîla-Symphonie* and the later *Et Expecto Resurrectionem Mortuorum*) would indeed fulfill certain of the extreme sonorous demands of Artaud's project with Varèse. Yet the intent was diametrically opposed, as Messiaen's goal was to incorporate these foreign effects into the Western musical canon, and thus expand it. To the contrary, Artaud wished to subvert those very same canons by introducing radically foreign musical forms which would continue to maintain their disruptive stylistic and metaphysical alterity opposed to cultural values.

An anecdote is revealing. The fact is that Artaud briefly worked with Messiaen in 1932, at the very moment that the former conceived his project with Varèse. This was during the rehearsals of *La pâtissière du village,* staged by Louis Jouvet. In regard to the need to create some nonmusical sound effects on the organ, Artaud's remarks about Messiaen were less than flattering:

I insist, moreover, that not being a musician myself, I can only convey ideas to the organist, yet he resists with all the force of his unconscious the idea of isolating non-musical sonorities; also, because of this tendency which he cannot overcome, his interpretation of even precise points is never what had been agreed upon. (3:322–23)

But due to rapid technical progress, contemporary musical events far outpaced the terms of this argument. The year 1948 also witnessed the birth of *musique concrète*, created by Pierre Schaeffer working in the studies of Radiodiffusion-télévision française. There was a continual perfecting of sound recording techniques – most notably the postwar development of magnetic tape – which permitted both the high quality recording of everyday sounds, as well as easier post-recording manipulation of the tape. Schaeffer utilized these possibilities to create a new sort of sound "object," not a musical composition but rather a musical drama of sound effects. Correspondingly, he argued that the playback capabilities of the gramophone would make it the most general musical instrument. (The 33 and 45 rpm speeds became the industrial standard in 1948.) It is of particular interest that the first such works of *musique concrète* were conceived to be broadcast on the radio. Early musical tape works were created in radio studios for the practical reason that such studios were among the very few places where musicians had access to the new recording technology; and radio management was motivated to occasionally make their facilities available because of the inherent cultural focus of radio's charter as a public service.

Musical vocabulary was vastly expanded by the introduction of sound recording on tape and the development of electronic sound sources, offering the following new musical possibilities: superposition of sounds; stereo and multitrack recording and mixing; distribution of sound through loudspeakers; canon or phasing consisting of two identical recordings played successively; new and complicated phrase lengths permitted by cutting and splicing; precise regulation of frequency and dynamics, and the consequent extension of such extreme dynamic and frequency ranges; rhythm patterns created by calculating duration by tape length; extreme speed changes; retrograde forms; loops; use of empty tape and white noise; transformations in sound attack and decay by means of tampering with transient noise, thanks to the precise and extremely brief switch-on and switch-off time of electroacoustic equipment; fading used to produce timbre transitions; sound filtering and ring modulation (and more recently computerized digital sampling) ultimately creating novel sounds.[17]

The earliest piece of *musique concrète* was Schaeffer's *Études aux chemins de fer* (*Railroad Study*), described as a "study of rhythm" rather than as a "still life with train," an abstract work rather than an evocation.[18] It was broadcast in May 1948 – a three minute piece of manipulated recordings, where a 78 rpm recording of trains was played back at 33 rpm, transforming the train sounds into those resembling a blast furnace. Later that year, on 5 October 1948, there was a broadcast of his "concert of noises," consisting of sounds derived from saucepans and piano chords. The piano was played by none other than the young Pierre Boulez, a student of Messiaen, and a future student of *musique concrète* in Schaeffer's electroacoustic studios at Radio France in 1951.

Boulez reveals the importance of Artaud's work for the musical experimentation of the epoch:

The name of Artaud immediately comes to mind when questions of vocal emission or the dissociation of words and their explosion are evoked; an actor and poet, he was naturally provoked by the material problems of interpretation, just like a composer who plays or conducts. I am not qualified to thoroughly investigate Artaud's language, but I can find in his writings the fundamental preoccupations of current music; having heard him read his own texts, accompanying them with screams, noises, rhythms, he showed us how to achieve a fusion of sound and word, how to splash out the phoneme when the word no longer can, in short, how to organize delirium. What nonsense and what an absurd alliance of terms, you'll say! Would you believe only in the vertigo of improvisation and the powers of an "elementary" sacralization? More and more, I imagine that to effectively create this we must consider delirium and, yes, organize it.[19]

Earlier, just after the creation of *To Have Done with the Judgment of God*, Boulez explains in "Propositions" (1948): "I think that music must be hysteria and collective bewitchment, violently present – following the direction of Antonin Artaud, and not in the sense of a simple ethnographic reconstitution in the image of civilizations more or less distant from us."[20] This position echoes one of Artaud's earliest aesthetic documents, the "Manifeste en langage clair" (Manifesto in Clear Language, 1925), a critique of discursive reason written at the time of Artaud's brief collaboration with the Surrealists:

This Meaning is lost in the disorder of drugs and appears profoundly intelligent in the contradictory phantasms of sleep. This Meaning is a conquest of the mind by itself, and although it is irreducible by reason, it exists, but only in the interior of the mind. It is order, it is intelligence,

it is the signification of chaos. But it does not accept this chaos as such,
it interprets it, loses it. It is the logic of Illogic. And this is to say every-
thing. My lucid unreason does not fear chaos. (1**:53)

These considerations of chaos were central to a key debate in the
history of modern music, and they were to be appropriated by
the most radical, antipodal exponents of contemporary music in
the 1950s, Pierre Boulez and John Cage. The debate would center
around the problem of musical logic and illogic, as manifested by
the role of chaos (chance, the aleatory) in musical composition
and performance. And it was precisely this question which would
be at the origins of the first contacts between Cage and Boulez, as
well as at the source of their eventual rupture.[21]

Boulez's theoretical and polemical statement on the role of
chance in music, written in 1957, is entitled "Alea."[22] Criticizing
what he terms the musical utilization of "chance by inadvertency,"
and "chance by automatism," Boulez insists on the appropriation
of "directed chance" – what we might term a "well-tempered
chance" – both at the moment of composition and of performance.
Thus chance need be absorbed in the musical work, rather than
control its production.

Though Artaud might have been the immediate inspiration for
this position, it was to Mallarmé that Boulez turned for a justifica-
tion of his poetics of controlled chance. (Boulez's *Pli selon pli* was a
musical "portrait," based on poems of Mallarmé.) And it was precisely in relation to interpretations stressing radically differing aspects of Mallarmé's writing that the rift between Boulez and Cage
developed. "Alea" ends with an evocation of Mallarmé's *Igitur:*

In an act where chance is at play, it is always chance that effects its own
Idea by affirming or denying itself. This negation or affirmation runs
aground before its very existence. It contains the Absurd – it implies it,
but in a latent state which hinders its existence: this permits Infinity to
exist.[23]

Boulez's conclusion is that the ultimate perfection-in-objectifica-
tion of music may occur through such a use of controlled chance –
appropriated in Boulez's total serialism, that is, his extension of the
organizational system of twelve-tone music to all musical parameters. This will entail "the only means to kill the Artist" faced with
the pure musical work.

Thus Mallarmé's entire work is imbued not only with the musical metaphor, but indeed with one of the most subtle and precise

senses of musication in modern French poetry. But this is a musicality radically divorced from expression. Though he claims that "every soul is a melody, which must be renewed,"[24] and "every soul is a rhythmic knot,"[25] considerations of the soul were in fact anathema for Mallarmé, since he rather sought a poetics where "the pure work implies the elocutionary disappearance of the poet, who cedes the initiative to words . . . replacing the perceptible respiration of the ancient lyrical breath or the personal enthusiastic direction of the sentence."[26] This elimination of expression, this rupture with mimesis culminating in the disappearance of the author, was for Mallarmé the key aesthetic function of the role of chance operations in art. But neither for Mallarmé nor for Boulez was this to be a "wild chance," as the former explains: "An arrangement of the book of verse appears innate or everywhere, and eliminates chance; this is still necessary, to omit the author. . . . "[27] Chance is to be organized within the artwork, where it shall ultimately disappear, along with all trace of the author, in the purity of a verse which bears its own perfection in its syntactic organization of words, rather than in its meaning. Such is poetry aspiring to the quality of music.

The seminal statement on the aesthetic role of chance is Mallarmé's ultimate work, *Un coup de dés jamais n'abolira le hasard*. The final line of this work is also cited as the final line of Boulez's 1951 text, "Moment de Jean-Sébastien Bach": "Toute Pensée émet un Coup de Dés" ("Every Thought Casts a Roll of the Dice"). Boulez's motivation is a critique of the state of contemporary music: "Amidst the appearances of logic from which we are rotting, apriorisms deprived of all critical spirit . . . let us finally provide its potential to what Mallarmé called 'Chance.'"[28] We might clarify what is at stake by creating a syllogism of the opening and closing sentences of the poem: "Un coup de dés jamais n'abolira le hasard. Toute pensée émet un coup de dés. Donc aucune pensée n'abolira le hasard" (A roll of the dice will never abolish chance. Every thought casts a roll of the dice. Therefore no thought will abolish chance). Every artwork is both the recipient and the producer of chance, where the aleatory is the web in which artist and spectator are mutually entangled. Can the same be said for the controlled chance of Boulezian musical composition?

During this same period, John Cage was concerned with related musical problems. The collaboration between Cage and Boulez began in 1949, when Boulez wrote an introductory text for a presentation of Cage's *Sonatas and Interludes*. Reciprocally, it was Cage who arranged for the U.S. premiere of Boulez's *Second Sonata* for piano, played by David Tudor. Indeed, it was through David Tudor's interest that Cage read Artaud (Cage especially gives credit to *The Theater and Its Double* for inspiring the famed 1952 multimedia event at Black Mountain College). The ensuing correspondence between Cage and Boulez was in part devoted to the problem of chance in music, and it soon became evident that their positions were diametrically opposed. Indeed, perhaps Boulez's most vicious critique of Cage was an oblique one, contained in the very last letter of their published correspondence, where Boulez writes: "The essential is, above all else, to create nonsense without any program!"[29] Yet by this time, their positions were totally incompatible, and, in any case, the great epoch of the aleatory was over.

Cage's concern with chance operations and the musical relevance of noise had its own history. Much of Cage's music of the 1930s and 1940s was created for the dance (especially that of Merce Cunningham). First of all, Cage argued that the only parameter shared by both dance and music is that of rhythm, thus all other parameters become incidental; furthermore, much of this dance music was percussive, and since percussion includes non-pitched sounds, it by definition potentially accepts any sound source. The possibility of freeing rhythm is thus at the origin of the notion of freeing timbre, thanks to the non-pitched aspect of many percussion instruments. Hence, for example, the creation of the prepared piano for Cage's 1938 composition *Bacchanale,* to accompany Syvilla Fort's dance piece of the same name. The insertion of objects such as wood screws, bolts, and weather stripping between the piano strings altered the timbre of the piano, disrupted the familiar consistency of the scales, and transformed the piano into a new sort of percussion instrument. Until that time, the only major work for percussion alone was Varèse's 1932 *Ionisation,* for thirteen players and thirty-seven percussion instruments; though this was a forerunner of electronic music due to its liberation of timbre and its sonic effects, it was nevertheless bound by Varèse's musical temperament and the limits of modernist musical sensibility.

Cage proposed a radically new interpretation of musical structure: arguing that as silence is the necessary coexistent of sound, and that of the four musical determinants (pitch, timbre, dynamics, duration) only duration is common to both sound and silence, musical structure should therefore be based on duration (and not harmony, as it was throughout the Western tradition to that moment). Thus he was no longer interested in conventional musical rhythms, but rather in the use of rhythm as a quantitative, metrical means of dividing and organizing musical time and structure. While Schoenberg's dodecaphonic revolution liberated dissonance from the need for resolution, Cage freed music from the need of considering the problem of dissonance.

But he did not stop there: he ultimately defined rhythm as pure and simple time lengths, implying that "rhythm is not at all something periodic and repetitive. It is the fact that something happens, something unexpected, something *irrelevant*."[30] Something, indeed *any sound event whatsoever*. Ultimately, rhythm is constituted by the temporal relations between any given events. As opposed to the permanent repetitive possibilities of written music, these Cagean innovations stressed the existential uniqueness of each individual moment, aiming at a music both immediate and ephemeral.

At first, in the 1940s, Cage utilized a system of arithmetic proportion to determine the rhythmic structure of his pieces; then, around 1949, he began to open these rhythmic structures to any content (the beginnings of the use of noise) and soon began to use chance operations to determine both rhythmic structure and content. Thus Cage's valorization of both noise and silence had strict musicological as well as pragmatic dance-related origins. In the 1942 text, "For More New Sounds," Cage praised the range of musical instruments in jazz, Oriental, and Latin music, advocating the use of such unconventional percussion instruments as automobile parts, pipe lengths, pieces of sheet metal, shells, whistles, and needles on records. He extrapolates these possibilities to their electronic limits, imagining a combination of such effects and the special sound effects of radio and film studios, utilizing devices created by acoustic engineers. Thus, along with Varèse, and following Russolo's 1913 pronouncements in "The Art of Noises," Cage at this point imagines of the possibility of electronic music, claiming that "many musicians, the writer included, have dreamed of compact technological boxes, inside which all audible sounds, including noise, would be ready to come forth at the command of the composer."[31]

It was at this time that Cage began to instantiate these phantasms of electric and electronic capabilities, by creating the first of his series of "imaginary landscapes." These pieces have the distinction of being among the first musical works where electronic and human capabilities are instantaneously mixed and performed. *Imaginary Landscape no. 1* (1939) is the first live work of electronic music: one microphone is used to pick up percussion sounds (derived from a Chinese cymbal and a piano played by either brushing the bass strings or by muting the strings by hand while playing on the keys), and the other microphone is used to pick up acoustic-research test recordings (electronic sounds) played on a turntable. The notation indicates rhythm (lifting the needle on and off the records) and speed changes on the turntable. *Imaginary Landscape no. 2* (1942) used a larger range of mechanical and electronic sounds, such as audio frequency oscillators, variable-speed turntables playing recordings of frequencies, and an amplified marimbula picked up with a contact microphone. A more sophisticated variant of these techniques is *Cartridge Music* (1960), whose score consists of transparent sheets upon which are printed various shapes used to control the performance, which entails the tapping or rubbing of objects (feathers, toothpicks, matches, piano wire) placed in a phonograph cartridge and objects (chairs, tables, wastepaper baskets) amplified by means of contact microphones. Changes of tone, amplitude, object replacement, and the use of repetitive loops are also controlled by the same means.[32] Here, noise becomes a signal, and the most intrusive, previously undesired aspects of recording and playback technology are brought into and highlighted within the musical realm.

Cage's "imaginary landscapes" were among the forerunners of virtual reality: existing on the tapes and in the circuits of recording and playback technology, and mixed with human percussive effects and aleatory recordings of quotidian sounds, these works represented a world transformed by the modulation of everyday sounds into their technical and musical counterparts. All sound – actual and potential; natural and artificial; live and recorded; past, present and future; private and public – is now accepted within the radically expanded musical canon, where music now permits the possibility of a totally "open work."

For Boulez, chance was to be controlled, just like every other parameter of music. For Cage, to the contrary, chance was to be given free rein, was to be allowed to control both composition and performance. Cage was particularly concerned with the multiplication of chance techniques which could serve as the origin of the artwork. Beginning with his first work composed utilizing chance operations, the piano piece entitled *Music of Changes* (1951) – based on the *I Ching* and deeply inspired by Zen Buddhism – Cage utilized chance operations to free himself from both pleasure and disgust. Thus Cage's chance operations are used to relinquish ego and authorship. Yet, if Cage's operations are mimetic, it is in imitation not of objects, but of the very processes of nature itself in its methods of operation. Cage was interested in process rather than product, in new percepts rather than new concepts; he wanted to set new processes in motion rather than create new musical structures. He explains in "Experimental Music":

And what is the purpose of writing music? One is, of course, not dealing with purposes but dealing with sounds. Or the answer must take the form of a paradox: a purposeful purposelessness or a purposeless play. This play, however, is an affirmation of life – not an attempt to bring order out of chaos nor to suggest improvements in creation, but simply a way of waking up to the very life we're living, which is so excellent once one gets one's mind and one's desires out of its way and lets it act of its own accord.[33]

The differences between Boulez and Cage are expressed by Cage, speaking of the role of the aleatory in Boulez:

Well, he used that word only to describe appropriate and correct chance operations, as opposed to those which seemed to him inappropriate or incorrect – mine! In fact, his chance operations fit into his compositions only as part of a drama. He very strictly distinguishes between determinate passages and "aleatory" passages in the same composition. As a whole, it becomes a drama between opposites: determinate vs. indeterminate.[34]

For Cage, the role of recording and chance operations allowed the entry of nonmusical sounds, of noise, into music, thus moving towards the elimination of the boundaries between life and art, very much in the Duchampian tradition. For Boulez, on the contrary, there is no place for noise in music: indeed, his total serialism (even including the limited role of aleatory operations) was intended to more fully order the linear structure of music as a pure work. To Boulez's equal distribution of chance operations on the fully determinate musical parameters of pitch, dynamics, duration, and rhythm, Cage opposes an unequal distribution of events within the musical context, both unforseeable and indeterminate. (Both of these techniques must be differentiated from Iannis Xenakis's "stochastic" compositions of the same epoch, developed according to probabilistic distributions of sounds.) Boulez absorbs chance in the work; Cage opens the work to the world through chance. Boulez aims at serial regulation, while Cage vaunts non-intention and "interpenetration without obstruction." Boulez wished to purify the musical idiom; Cage wished to raise music to the conditions of theater, to nature, to life itself – in all its disequilibrium, splendor, and joy.

In "For More New Sounds" (1942) Cage calls for the organization of sound effects with their expressive rather than representational qualities in mind.[35] Later, even the expressive aspects of sound are to be eliminated so as to let the sounds exist without any egological intervention — or at least as little as possible. Consider Cage's quip against Varèse, claiming that he is in fact an artist of the past, since "rather than dealing with sounds as sounds, he deals with them as Varèse."[36] Yet we must say that, even given the use of silence, noise, indetermination, chance – all intended to avoid the intervention of the human ego in letting sounds be themselves – Cage's compositional frames are a well-defined means to organize and give style to such noise, sound, and music. Ironically, the ego returns through the institution of this style as a coherent deformation of the modern musical field.

In 1952 Merce Cunningham choreographed the first dance to a work of *musique concrète,* Pierre Schaeffer's *Symphonie pour un homme seul* (*Symphony for a Single Man*), which was originally produced in 1949, and later turned into a ballet by Maurice Béjart. This piece used both pitched sounds and assorted noises, categorized by Schaeffer as *human sounds* (breathing, vocal fragments, shouting, humming, whistled tunes) and *nonhuman sounds:* (footsteps, knocking on doors, percussion, prepared piano, orchestral instruments). Thus, the earliest utilization of tape-recorded sounds in music opened up the musical field to nonmusical sounds, that is, to noise. Cage, who met Schaeffer in Paris in 1949, criticized his work as being too concerned with relationships, organization, and standard problems of tonality. Cage's response was *William's Mix.*

In *William's Mix* (1952), Cage used both recorded music and noise.[37] This tape-collage piece included the following categories of taped concrete and electronic sounds (taken from a stock of about 600 recordings), cut up into short fragments, cataloged according to pitch, timbre, and loudness, and edited at random according to operations of the *I Ching:* city sounds, country sounds, electronic sounds, manually produced sounds (including music),

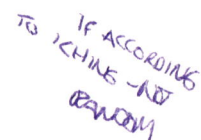

wind-produced sounds (including songs), and small sounds requiring amplification in order to be heard. To realize the radical paradigm-shift established by such music, consider it from the technical point of view. Imagine the impossible job of working in a recording studio listening to master pressings for imperfections, where the task is not to hear the music, but the noise. How could we check recordings of *musique concrète* or of Cage's *William's Mix,* for example? Such a work as *William's Mix* instantiates Cage's quasi-Dadaist or Surrealist theory of "aggregates," that is, the juxtaposition of disparate aural objects in musical space. Furthermore, the montage of sounds in turn evokes the larger scale possibility of a montage, or perhaps a palimpsest, of various media.

Cage was later to extrapolate the aggregate theory in order to create the juxtaposition of different media. This sort of "mix" was exemplified in the legendary mixed-media, interdisciplinary performance at Black Mountain College – including music, poetry, dance, lectures, film, slides – conceived by Cage, and performed by Merce Cunningham, David Tudor, Mary Caroline Richards, Charles Olson, and Robert Rauschenberg. Articulated initially in the context of experimental music, Cage's aesthetic rationale – that of a purposeful purposelessness or a purposeless play, derived from a combination of Duchamp and Zen – pertains, mutatis mutandis, to all the arts.[38] Cage broke down the barriers between life and art following Duchamp's invention of the Readymade: "He simply found that object, gave it his name. . . . Say it's not a Duchamp. Turn it over and it is. . . . Therefore, everything seen – every object, that is, plus the process of looking at it – is a Duchamp."[39] This paved the way for the arts of Assemblage, Happenings, Mixed-Media, Combines, Pop Art, Minimalism, Conceptual Art, and so forth. As Cage wrote in *Empty Words:* "Languages becoming musics, musics becoming theaters; performances; metamorphoses."[40]

The ultimate extrapolations of Cage's position – whether we deem it revolutionary, iconoclastic, nihilistic, or simply logical and musical – lead to the use of pure noise and pure silence, the latter exemplified in perhaps his most famous work, *4′ 33″* (1952), consisting of four minutes and thirty-three seconds of silence scored originally for pianist, and later revised as being scored for "undetermined force." This work – a proof that silence never actually exists at the auditory level – is a way of letting the ambient concert hall sounds and noises become, if not the music itself (since the score does not contain indications of noises), at least the center of attention. The studies dealing with Cage and silence are vast, and the reader is referred to Cage's own book of essays, *Silence,* for clarification. Let it suffice in this context to cite Cage's earliest thoughts on the matter, "A Composer's Confessions," written well before the composition of *4' 33",* in what has become a crucial year for the history of radiophony, 1948. He explains one of his current musical desires, which he admits might seem absurd, but about which he claims to be quite serious:

> *To compose a piece of uninterrupted silence and sell it to Muzak Co. It will be 3 or 4½ minutes long – those being the standard lengths of "canned" music – and its title will be* Silent Prayer.*[41]*

The musical trajectory of this silence maintains an increasingly richer future.

Yet the antipodal limits of noise and silence are not so very distant from each other. One sound effects engineer offers a technical trick which reveals an entire metaphysics of sound, silence, and recording. He explains that "a most uncanny yet effective impression of brooding silence can be obtained between the individual portions of activity by recording *very* faintly, the sound of distant voices alone."[42] From Pascal's admission that "the eternal silence of these infinite spaces frightens me," to the "color of silence" which haunts every recording studio in a different manner, to the anechoic chamber in which Cage discovered that there is no such thing as pure silence (since one always hears the coursing of the blood and the hum of the nervous system), we each discover our own silence, we each recreate silence as a metaphor. From noise to silence, from panic to quiescence, from catastrophe to calm: the very existence of silence both depends upon noise *and* permits noise to exist.

Cage's major radiophonic work, and one of his most celebrated performances, is *Imaginary Landscape no. 4* (1951), where silence arrived in ironic stealth. This work of *bruitage* – where radios are transformed into musical instruments – entails the diametrical opposite of those standard splicing techniques used to create ideal sound configurations. This piece for twelve radios—a do-it-yourself composition determined by chance operations of the *I Ching* – demands two operators per radio, controlling changes of amplitude from *ppppp* to *fffff,* of frequency settings spanning the dial, and of duration.[43] The work is thus indeterminate regarding both composition and performance. It was first performed in 1951 at the McMillan Theater at Columbia University, "conducted" by

Cage himself. One auditor recounts that due to awkward scheduling, the performance didn't begin until 11:30 P.M., a time at which, in that epoch, there was practically nothing on the radio. The result seemed to some an unfortunate mix of static and silence; yet others recognized it as the most fortunate serendipity, prefiguring Cage's inventions of the use of noise and silence in musical composition. True to form, Cage claims that he had indeed foreseen the fragility of this work and that the radios performed perfectly that evening. Since the piece was composed to avoid the direct intervention of the ego in performance, any results whatsoever would have to be accepted, including, of course, the low dynamic levels of that particular performance.[44]

This attempt at a noisy collage of music, voice, and the assorted sounds of commercial radio – a music created with radiophonic detritus – is, like the later *William's Mix,* made possible by the radical consideration of the radio as active musical agent, and not merely as a passive transmitter.[45] According to Cage, silence is indeterminate noise. We might presume that Cage was inspired to silence, to the many possible silences, by this error of timing. In any case, the desire to include the radical contingency of the world – the "real" world, the recorded world, the radiophonically represented world – in music was met with an emblematic failure. The scheduling "error" has informed the creative thought of a generation. Sometimes the world which we anticipate or desire is missing; sometimes that which we need to define our imagination – in this case, a montage of mediatic, radiophonic excerpts – escapes us. One limit of nonsense, *noise,* gives way to another, *silence.*

In conclusion, I should like to fill these silences with perhaps the most noisy and celebratory of Cage's sounds, unrealized as it may be. Cage wished to create a work using the thunderclaps from Joyce's *Finnegans Wake.* Listen to the first of these cosmic peals of thunder: *bababadalgharaghtakamminarronnkonnbronntonnerronntuonnthunntrovarrhounawnskawntoohoohoordenenthurnuk!* Cage explained: "I would like to have some equipment made that would be attached to the throats of the chorus members so that when they sing *Thunderclaps,* their sound would fill up the envelopes of actual thunderclaps."[46] He wished to mix the natural and the human, sacred and profane, the literary and the musical, sense and nonsense. Recording stylizes the sounds of the world, outdoing nature in dramatic quality. Yet Cage wished to go beyond nature, realism, expression – to let sound be, to let silence resound.

CHAPTER 3

The cosmos is a rigged theater. — Antonin Artaud

Diderot's *Paradoxe sur le comédien* (1773) provides one of the origins of the modern theory of theater and acting: a psychological, narrative theater endowed with the rationalist exigencies expressed by the *Encyclopédie* that Diderot edited. This is to be a theater radically divorced from life, as is made evident by the debate between the two interlocutors. In a passage which curiously prefigures Artaud's theatrical innovations, the creative virtues of spontaneity are proposed:

But if a crowd of people gathered in the street all of a sudden displayed their natural sensibilities because of some catastrophe, each in his own

manner and without any concerted action, they would create a mar-
velous spectacle, a thousand precious models for sculpture, painting, music
and poetry.[1]

This proposal is immediately discounted by Diderot's discursive
stand-in, the first interlocutor, as being the antithesis of the essence
of theater, where great actors need be moved by cool, insensitive
judgement, and where the free rein of sensibility impedes such
judgement.

Compare Artaud's description, in *The Theater and Its Double,*
of an archetypal, paradigmatic scene displaying a manifestation of
the "theater of cruelty." Writing against Racine, he could equally be
speaking against Diderot:

Imbued with the idea that the crowd thinks first of all with its senses, and
that it is absurd to address oneself first of all to its understanding, as does
the psychological theater, the Theater of Cruelty proposes to resort to mass
spectacle; to seek in the agitation of huge masses, convulsed and hurled
one against the other, a bit of that poetry found in festivals and crowds on
those days, all too rare nowaday, when people pour out into the streets.
(4:102)[2]

For Artaud, actors must be like "victims burnt at the stake, signal-
ing through the flames," and the theater should coincide with life,
and attain "that sort of fragile and shifting hearth which forms
never touch" (4:18). The actor is no longer guided or inspired by
another's text, a scenario; rather, it is life itself in all its vicissitudes
and terrors that inspires, and is articulated by, the actor.

For Diderot, to the contrary, the actor is "a fabulous puppet,
for whom the poet holds the strings, and determines the essential
shaping of his part." In his critique of "sensibility," the first interlocutor offers the following definition, which should provide us
with an appropriate segué into our consideration of Artaud, who
represents all that is anathema to the tradition spawned by Diderot, that is, to the very tradition of Western theater.

Sensibility, according to the only accepted meaning of this term up to the
present, is, it seems to me, that disposition attendant to the weakness of
organs, owing to the mobility of the diaphragm, the vivacity of the imagi-
nation and the delicateness of the nerves, which disposes one to sympath-
ize, to shudder, to admire, to fear, to get flustered, to cry, to faint, to shake,
to flee, to scream, to lose one's reason, to exaggerate, to scorn, to disdain, to
have no precise idea of the true, the good and the beautiful, to be unjust, to
be mad.[3]

Does this not foreshadow the "affective athleticism" demanded of the actor by Artaud in that radical manifesto of theater and of life, *The Theater and Its Double,* where sensibility is the very foundation of existence? Artaud bemoans the fact that it "is not even an organ, but a monstrous abstraction that speaks: actors in France no longer know how to do anything but speak" (4:164). While speech in the Western theater has been reduced to psychological effects, the theater of cruelty would directly affect the entire human organism.

But, for the moment, it is the ultimate effect mentioned in Diderot's text with which we must be concerned: madness. Criticizing Shakespearian theater and the notion of art-for-art's-sake, with its separation of life and art, Artaud argues that "we see, nevertheless, all too many signs that all that sustains our lives no longer holds, that we are all mad, despondent and ill" (4:93). Guided by a hyperbolic biographism, this "illness," this "madness," is the central metaphor of *The Theater and Its Double,* where the plague is utilized as the most appropriate symbol for the theater of cruelty, seen as a communicable delirium, a delirium which we, the spectators are invited to share, a theater in which we are invited to participate (4:33).

The presumed insufficiencies of language have haunted writers throughout the ages. Indeed, at the basis of Nietzsche's critique of Western epistemology and morality is a linguistic diatribe against conceptuality. In "On Truth and Lie in an Extra-Moral Sense," he explains:

Every concept originates through our equating what is unequal. No leaf ever wholly equals another, and the concept "leaf" is formed through an arbitrary abstraction from these individual differences, through forgetting the distinctions. . . . What then is truth? A mobile army of metaphors, metonyms, anthropomorphisms – in short, a sum of human relations, which have been enhanced, transposed, and embellished poetically and rhetorically, and which after long use seem firm, canonical, and obligatory to a people: truths are illusions about which one has forgotten that this is what they are.[4]

Jean Dubuffet – who in 1945 began his research into *Art Brut,* those rare, radically inventive, or bizarre artistic works of people situated at the margins of culture – the mad, the isolated, the eccentric – established the parallel notion of *écrits bruts* to account for those texts which do not fall under our standard cultural purview.[5] Here, the standard genres and narrative forms of literary and discursive writing are overturned; vocabulary is reinvented, syntax shattered, and orthography transformed. Dubuffet's rationale parallels that of Nietzsche:

And yet we also have the feeling that that the repertory of words utilized in each of our languages is extremely narrow in relation to the innumerable apprehensions of thought, and that each of these words suffers a great poverty in their abstract status, in order to translate the particular situations of each designated thing and the associations which link thought to it. It is said that there are fifteen different ways of saying "camel" in Arab, and there are without a doubt as many ways of saying "seal" or "snow" in Eskimo. But do only fifteen suffice? A hundred times a hundred thousand are needed. And in this regard, we still wouldn't have enough. For thought is in motion, while words are inert bodies. What we need is words in motion.[6]

Consider, for example, the writing of Gaston Duf (discovered by Dubuffet). Also known as Gaston the Zoologist, Duf was interned in a French psychiatric asylum in 1940, where he began to paint and write. Observe his transformations of the word *rhinocéros:*

Rinâûçêrshôse
Rhin'-Oçêrhâûshe
Rin'-hâûçêr-hâûs'he
Lin'-hôçêr'-hâûs
Irâûçerâûse
Rônâûsêrôse
R'-inôçêrôse
Rhin'-hhhâûçêrôs
Rinôsâirâûs[7]

The liberatory, potentially subversive, aspects of such orthographic gestures are apparent. Roland Barthes thematizes and generalizes the problem in terms of "a sort of drunkenness, of a baroque jubilation, which bursts forth across orthographic 'aberrations,'" arising from the writer's phantasms as they free orthography from its normative rules, thus creating a new means of expression.[8] Perhaps, suggests Barthes, such aberrant writing proceeds under the dictates not of standard linguistic laws, but rather according to the mysterious, non-thetic commandments of the writer's private history, of the writer's own body.

These verbigerations, this logorrhea, though nonsensical and non-referential, exists within an ancient yet thoroughly marginalized branch of literary history: that of the pure verbal fantasies and the irrational poetry of late Latin, deriving from hyperbolic modes of expression such as the *fatrasie, soties de menus-propos, coq-à-l'âne, galimatias, baguenaudes,* through the *amphigouris* of the eighteenth century.[9] The anglophone branch of this tradition culminates in Lewis Carroll's famous poem "Jabberwocky," though a vast amount of less well-known but not necessarily lesser works exists. The major modernist francophone manifestation appropriating this tradition is the work of the contemporary French playwright Valère Novarina.[10]

Anti-theater has become a staple of modernist drama. Yet, following Artaud's theatrical and poetic innovations, Novarina has established a theatrical practice that leads well beyond the theatrical, directly into the morass of the body, which for Novarina is ultimately indistinguishable from the extreme possibilities of language itself. His theatrical manifesto, "Letter to the Actors," exhorts the actor to reach and express this sub-liminal, corporeal core of speech. He proposes a use of the voice which harkens back to Artaud's own transformation of the vocal arts:

Mouth, anus. Sphincters. Round muscles closing our holes. The opening and the closing of the word. Attack cleanly (teeth, lips, muscled mouth) and finish cleanly (cut off the air). Stop cleanly. Chew and eat the text. A blind spectator should be able to hear it crunched and swallowed, to ask himself what is being eaten over there, on stage. What are they eating? They're eating themselves? Chewing or swallowing. Mastication, sucking, swallowing. Pieces of the text must be bitten off, viciously attacked by the female eaters (lips, teeth); other pieces must be quickly gulped down, swallowed, gobbled up, breathed in, guzzled. Eat, gulp, eat, chew, dry lung, chew, masticate, cannibal![11]

Novarina recreates the very structure of work and the sense of life itself by sheer logological proliferation, as in the ornithological inventions with which he concludes *Le Discours aux animaux* (*Discourse to the Animals*). Like a delirious, linguistically deranged Saint Francis, the narrator finds himself in the forest one day, with 1,111 different birds at his feet, which he names in an onomastic frenzy, one by one, beginning with:

la limnote, la fuge, l'hypille, le ventisque, le lure, le figile, le lépandre, la galoupe, l'ancret, le furiste, le narcile, l'aulique, la gymnestre, la louse, le drangle, le ginel, le sémelique, le lipode, l'hippiandre, le plaisant, la cadmée, la fuyau, la gruge, l'étran, le plaquin, le dramet, le vocifére, le lèpse, l'useau, la grenette, le galéate . . .[12]

These lists in the form of a litany have as their goal, according to Novarina, to "repeat the names unto a whirling drunkenness,"[13] a practice comparable to Artaud's incantatory, exorcistic use of glossolalic language in his theater of cruelty. The recitations of such litanies constitute a primal creative act. Many of Novarina's nominations are utilized only once; many of his "characters" speak only once; most never speak, or even appear, at all. They exist only through their names: existence is reduced to nomination, to pure connotation, without any possibility of description (as in *Le Drame de la vie* (*The Drama of Life*)). Every such unique name is a *hapax legomenon*, a term existing but once in a language, without origin or end, afterwards forever lost. This proliferation of names and words coincides with a reduction of bodies and entails a (perhaps compensatory) multiplication of grammatical moods and tenses:

The antepositive accords in number with the gender of the preposition which its verb complements; in the equalitive mode, as well as in the depreciative mode, the object of the subject remains blank. Recite the six modes that exist! The optional, the dictative, the subodorative, the injunctive, the inactive, the dodecational. The mode of separation is separative; the mode of options is the optional. Sixteen tenses exist while there is still time: the distant present, the advanced future, the inactive present, the disactive past, the more-than-present, its projective past, the posterior past, the worse-than-past, the never possible, the completed future, the terminated past, the possible anterior, the future posterior, the more-than-lost, the completative, the attentive.[14]

Don't we need an indefinite number of novel tenses and grammatical modes, as vast as the rhetorical possibilities being rediscovered by today's theoretical linguistics? Such aberrations reveal the madness of the imagination, the manifestation of difference in extremis. As each vocal monster bears a totally idiosyncratic structure, new grammatical, rhetorical, and poetic models are needed to describe such irregular, eccentric, heteromorphic discursive patterns.[15]

As the thrust of the new manifesto of a corporeal theater constituted by the "Letter to the Actors," Novarina demands, in the imperative mood: "Articulatory cruelty, linguistic carnage."[16] Everything that destroys or circumvents our linguistic habits is valorized: errors, slurs, babble, lapsus, agrammaticisms, malapropisms, aphasia, and whatever other effects – psychopathological or quotidian – loosen the tongue, worsen speech, fracture the word. Believing in the interlocutory presence of the lived body, Novarina is truly a man of the theater, and he consequently provides a critique of present-day mainstream radio:

They work night and day with immense teams and enormous financial means: a cleansing of the body in sound recording, a toilet of the voice, filtering, tapes edited and carefully purified of all laughs, farts, hiccoughs, salivations, respirations, of all the slag that marks the animal, material nature of the words that come from the human body.[17]

These considerations serve as a prolegomena to Novarina's own radiophonic production. For while his theatrical production is based upon the primacy of corporeal effects and strategies, this in no way precludes the possibility of what he terms "the separated theater," literally a "theater of the ears." Witness this description of his own inner speech:

Uproar, cavalcades, parades, entry of words, exit of words: they are engendered, they reproduce themselves. Now and then, language exists outside of bodies, without man, outside of the world. Lightening, discharges, perturbations, explosions: it's like a voyage of voices, outside of the normal paths of communicative language. A non-figurative, rupestral, parietal theater. No characters, but inhabited costumes, and an entire bestiary of siamese, hydras, solitary heads, bodies with a thousand heads, heads with a thousand mouths, flying members. Before, behind, below and above, we hear the noise of a future tribe, fossilized sounds, a stratum of resurging words, the resurrection of names, the resurrection of sounds, all in a space without dimension, in a space with a hundred dimensions, as if perspective had disappeared, as if something had fallen. Something fell. I am no longer the master of the book, he who releases its meaning, the reader's guide, he who directs the reader, but rather someone who undertakes the voyage along with him. I know no more than he about the book, unless it be that I too must descend along with him.[18]

The realization of this psychic soundscape occurred radiophonically, in Novarina's production of *Le théâtre des oreilles* (*The Theater of the Ears*) in June 1980 for France Culture. (And we might note that it was commissioned by René Farabet for the Atelier de Création Radiophonique which he directs – and it was Farabet who first broadcast Artaud's *To Have Done with the Judgment of God* in the early 1970s for this same radio workshop.) The broadcast is outlined in the following text, which is the letter (1980) that Novarina sent Farabet as the proposal for this emission:

Theater of the Ears: the work of a single man. Theater of the Ears: an opera by a man confined. An opera within a single man.

Alone in the studio for over two hours, he will be the only source of sounds, noises, words, the only living being still heard beating. He will walk into the studio alone, he will sing within it as in his own tomb, he will speak as one who speaks after his own death.

A rhythmic self-portrait: an x-ray. The actor x-rayed with all the rhythms he has eaten. Writing with music below; sounds with words within. X-rays, like those bark paintings of Arnhem Land, an organic music from within, not musical but muscular, like a dance that cannot be seen.

Self-penetration, self-hypnosis, a descent into the sonorous body, a dance within the ears, a song of separated members – he shall descend into the animal's soul, for he seeks an animal within an animal, an animal within his animal in the profoundest depths, where there exists the negative rhythm of all spoken words, like a finger's trace, a negative hand, a rhythmic scar at the core, a mark, a fossil sound, a negative music, the negative of words.

Dance of the deaf, literature of the caves, radio of within, parietal music, voice of the dead, descent into tongues, *languish* in *fa* in *la* in *fa* in *la*, the calling of names, a list of words never pronounced, glossolalia, glossophagia: a man will give himself over to the task of speaking all musics, of playing all languages.

Musical gestures, muscular birth, birth of the voice, sonorous acts, rhythmic beats, stupid refrains, verbal crimes: by grimaces and by elevations, falls and levitations, holy and comic – always more holy, always more comic – he shall rise and descend, he shall sing in silence, he shall dance immobile, until tongues and musics descend upon him.

Alone for hours, he will recite the list of people, he will recite the list of all mankind: omians, ominidians, oliminitudians, umians, ulimians, unaninians, urians, onanidians, ulimilitudians, onians, unanians, onaninians – he will touch the instruments for the first time, enter into the fabric of the word, descend deeper into the emission, into the hospital of voices, he will touch all the instruments one by one.

A concert without a conductor, an opera without a head, a music without baton, an asocial orchestra. Murmuring to itself like an isolated tribe, singing the chants of civilization to one alone, speaking all the noises, pronouncing all the sounds of a solitary society. Jettisoned sounds, dances, uproars, chants of consonents, *fa*, noises of vowels, nontympanic music, spermatic music. Sing like someone apart.

But it will be necessary to methodically number all of this, fold all of this, separate all of this, to classify, split, set it all in divided music, on two tapes, on two tracks, always double, because man has two arms, two heels, two feet, two hands, two ears.

I would like to enter into the State radio – which is like a theater where everyone stiffens up, sits upright, wants to win over voices – to devote myself fully to it, lose voice, give up my language, create something that falls, show a speaking man who falls, reveal the speaking being, create something that descends, traverses, make something fall, during two hours, give up speaking, descend upon my sonorous shipwreck. It's suicide by waves: a man who disappears while speaking. Something that speaks to nobody. He's a man who disappears while speaking. I would like to make music which passes away, which nobody can ever remember or play.

Who are his precursors in this carnal quest, this disruption of the French language, this reconciliation of word and body? The *Bible* (for its genealogical litanies and archetypical creations); Rabelais (for the sheer inventiveness of his language, the concerted use of the cadences and accents of quotidian speech, and his carnivalesque upheavals of cultural values); La Fontaine (specifically for the corporeal and imaginative possibilities implied by animals that speak, as well as for the perfection of his phrasing); Blaise Pascal (because of his theological mysteries); Victor Hugo (for his celebration of slang and jargon); Alfred Jarry (for the hyperbolic derision, cynicism and obscene farce of his pataphysical theater, the violent comedy of his Grand Guignolesque character Ubu, and his scabrous condemnation of contemporary mores); Raymond Roussel (for the abstract word play and linguistic systematization of this *fou littéraire*); Artaud (not only in his theory and practice of a "theater of cruelty," but perhaps even more so through the linguistic madness of the *Cahiers de Rodez* and also in the final works accomplished upon his return to Paris just before his death, such as *Artaud le mômo, Ci-gît, Suppôts et suppliciations,* and *Pour en finir avec le jugement de dieu*); Jean Dubuffet (through his search for the diverse excesses within *écrits bruts* – enunciations no longer dissociated from our corporeal functions, nor from our libidinal impulses). This very list is in itself Rabelaisian, indicating the manifest difficulties and rewards in reading and translating the works of

Novarina. In fact, rather than merely summing up an aberrant tradition, it might be said that Novarina represents the contemporary French language in its extreme state of mutation, distortion, and transformation.

Such linguistic inventions and appropriations as those of Novarina – shattering the quotidian flow of language in a rare outburst of non-sense at all levels of discourse: phonetic, orthographic, lexical, grammatical, and narrative – were not achieved without consideration of the psychopathology of language. Do these examples of linguistic deformation and creation constitute mere idiolalia or idioglossia (i.e., a mispronunciation so extreme that the person seems to be speaking a language of one's own), or are they the creations of idiolects bordering on private language? Perhaps the best explanation would be in terms of Michel Thévoz's notion of "sphinx-words" which simultaneously stress their mystery, uninterpretability, and hermeticism.[19] This is precisely the point where the reader, always potentially a hermeneut, must stop making sense in order to read and hear the text.

Examine a brief text by Jeanne Tripier (one of the *écrivains bruts* read by Novarina), a spiritualist medium incarcerated in the asylum of Maison-Blanche near Paris in 1934, diagnosed as having chronic hallucinatory psychosis, psychic excitation, logorrhea, megalomania. The following glossographia is part of a spiritualist message: "AXYZZKXY. toyou govistoricotoloya sisquisi pédro Géolio bgdqxasivdqg üobodico siscotoya dico puelsicofloye abdgqgxyzz, iabcqvxtzavryisqui bibicotogoldano."[20] Her mediumistic transcriptions and associations included contacts with and messages from Zed Zed Zibodandez (the Universal Dictator), Sainte Thérèse, Marie-Antoinette, Lucifer I, Morphée des Catacombes, and many other astral luminaries and fluidic doubles, especially Joan of Arc, with whom Tripier identified. She believed herself to be Joan of Arc's missionary, and in fact identified with that prophet, signing many of her "interplanetary communications" *Sainte Jeanne Tripier Jeanne d'Arc*. These messages thus describe a closed circuit of communication, a solipsistic discourse. We cannot differentiate Tripier's mediumistic expression from her psychopathological symptoms: it is only within different discursive, hermeneutic contexts that these distinctions may be established. The diagnosis of mental illness must have other than simply textual sources; and yet, what expression is ultimately not textual? It is this vicious hermeneutic circle which establishes the conundrum of all reading: the never-fixed ratio of autobiographically based hermeneutics to textually based interpretation differs from work to work. But in no case can one be reduced to the other: the differences between hermeneutics (the relations between life and text) and interpretation (the intra- and intertextual relations) create levels or interfaces, and not origins, of meaning.

The issue of religious, mediumistic, and psychopathological glossolalia (babble) is exemplary. The procedure of discovery and appropriation is twofold: while modernist procedures opened the possibilities of accepting nonclassical forms into art, aesthetically attuned psychiatrists and linguists disclosed their own discoveries of such forms, making them available for transmogrification into the artistic realm. Glossolalia – which entails the enunciation of the pure signifier, the refusal of meaning, and the reduction of speech to the pure voice, of language to the body – manifested that foregrounding of the signifier which is now a central tenet of modernism. In turn, the valorization of such forms in early modernist poetic experimentation – Italian Futurism's *Parole in libertà,* Russian Futurism's *zaum,* Tristan Tzara's dadaist experiments, Kurt Schwitter's *Merz,* Surrealist automatism; and later in *Lettrisme, CoBrA,* the writings of Henri Michaux, Gaston Chaissac, Raymond Queneau and *Ou.Li.Po., Sound Poetry,* Dubuffet, Novarina, and others – all championed the interest of glossolalia as poetic devices. A celebrated example would be Tzara's sound poem, "Toto-vaca" (which might be compared with Artaud's glossolalia):

Ka tanga te kivi
kivi
Ka tangi te moho
moho
Ka tangi te tike
Ka tangi te tike
tike
he poko anahe
to tikoko tikoko
haere i te hara[21]

Or children's comptines, much neglected in this context, also provide a rich source for such linguistic, purely phonetic invention:

Emelesi
Peteri, Petera
Rupetera
Pétecnol[22]

The shift in discursive formations established by the intersection of linguistics and modernist poetry in such works as Saussure's study of anagrams, the Moscow linguistic circle's relations to Russian Futurist poetry, and psychoanalytically oriented literary theory, permitted the incorporation of psychopathological symptomatology into aesthetic production, broadening the range of aesthetic possibility. In turn, these broader aesthetic criteria permitted the very productions of the insane to be deemed art, an aesthetic paradigm shift originally championed by the Expressionists and Surrealists, and one which ultimately permitted Dubuffet's researches into *Art Brut* and *écrits bruts*. A final stage of this process entails the investigators themselves creating art that follows these new linguistic structures and events, such as Michaux's and Dubuffet's literary and plastic works.

The desire to inflect, indeed transform, writing by utilizing quotidian, phonetically transcribed vocal patterns led Dubuffet to create what he termed his "Jargon, frénésies," literary texts such as *LER DLA CANPANE, ANVOUAIAJE,* and *LABONFAM ABEBER. LER DLA CANPANE* ("L'air de la campagne"), for example, begins: "SQON NAPELE LEPE ISAJE SAVEDIR LA CANPANE IARIIN QI MANBETE COMSA LACANPANE." (Ce qu'on appelle le paysage, ça veut dire la campagne, rien qui embête comme ça, la campagne.")[23] The roots of this procedure – evident in the earliest instances of French literature, such as the *Serment de Strasbourg,* and highly valorized in writings from Rabelais through Céline – are also to be found in certain examples of *écrits bruts,* such as the following text by a psychiatric patient named Annette:

> *la porte je*
> *festrme mon kalendri*
> *ié j'ouvre me di qant*
> *nou nesttron avestq*
> *no z'estl vint trw*
> *a aout dimanche*
> *s philippe bén je*
> *chanteré*
> *papiion vole vole voole*
> *vole don papiion sur la*
> *flere tu te poze rose . . .*[24]

Consider also the *écrits bruts* of Samuel D., whose orthographic declensions give an indication of yet another manner of creating these linguistic anomalies: "Je suis zodiaquismeuraux, zodiaqeulismeuraux; zodiaquestrismeuraux, zodiaquestrelismeuraux. ZODIAQUIEMEURAUX. – ZODIAQUELISMEURAUX. ZODIAQUESTRISMEURAUX. ZODIAQUESTRELISMEURAUX."[25] Furthermore, Samuel D.'s lexical innovations, syntactically reduced to monoremes, break with all possible narrative sense:

Chevalo. Vélo. moto. auto. Traino. Tramevo. Bato. Plano: Sénor. Doctor. Rector. Royer. Firmor. Factor. Chevalelo. Vélelo. Motelo. Autelo. Tranelo. Tramvelo. Batelo. Planelo: Pénoral. Sénoral. Doctorel. Rectorel. Royorel. Firmorel. Pastor. – mission comission. mis. comis. missaire. comissaire. missionaire. comissionaire[26]

The linguistic and psychological characteristics of *écrits bruts* may be considered in either psychopathological or aesthetic terms. Jean Bobon, in *Introduction historique à l'étude des néologismes et des glossolalies en psychopathologie* (*Historical Introduction to the Study of Neologisms and Glossolalia in Psychopathology*), provides a compendium of the varied linguistic effects of mental illness: neologisms, paralogisms, agrammatism, paragrammatism, glossolalia, glossomania, dysphasia, dyslogia, paraphasia, neologia, schizophasia, paragraphism, and so on. Indeed, one might go so far as to presume a different linguistic disorder for each possible rhetorical trope and figure! Michel Thévoz, revealing his antipsychiatric sentiment, spoofs these categorizations:

Mallarmè's writing is characterized by atelophemia, idiophemia, leipophemia, paraphemia, stereophemia *and* apatelophrasia, *while that of Joyce manifests tendencies of* polyphemia, spasmophemia, tachyphemia, dramatophrasia, embolophrasia, cataphrasia, echophrasia, planophrasia *and* schizophrasia. *In fact, we see that in terms of neologisms and "jargonographia," the psychiatrists hardly lag behind their patients.*[27]

At one of the culminations of modernism, linguistics and poetry converge in Roman Jakobson's study of the two basic types of aphasic language disturbances, similarity and contiguity disorders.[28] *Similarity disorders* affect the lexical selection of linguistic units, where each word is dependent upon syntax for meaning. A word out of context has no meaning or referential stability. This is a discourse that approaches a truly private language, a pure ideo-

lect. *Contiguity disorders* affect the syntactic rules of sentence organization, such that words bear their own meaning, and sentence
structure tends to disintegrate, resulting in chaotic word order and
the use of monoremes (one word sentences, such as those in the
écrits bruts of Samuel D.), leading to the disintegration of words
into pure phonemes. It is ultimately manifested as *aphasia universalis,* the complete loss of language. The latter may be grasped, in
the final analysis, as a potential manifestation of what the artist
Arnulf Rainer terms *Katatonenkunst,* or catatonic art.

Yet how must such "psychopathological" manifestations or
works be treated? Do they indeed fall within the category of literature (modernist or otherwise)? Must they be relegated simply to
the realm of psychiatric symptomatology, or is there a unique category within which they must be considered? In "Writing and Madness," Octave Mannoni argues (in the context of Daniel Paul Schreber's *Memoirs of My Nervous Illness,* the book on which Freud based
his theory of psychosis) that the writings of the mad constitute a
unique literary genre. Yet even within this genre, we must at least
distinguish between those works written during the period of madness, and those other, albeit rare ones, written in retrospect, after
the illness has passed (as is Schreber's case). The latter sort often
tends toward a theological narrative account, while the former
tends toward the fragmentation of the linguistic system. The difference between the original mad event and its retrospective account
is the fact that, as Mannoni explains:

*What gets lost is whatever agency may be capable of critiquing the orig-
inally given hallucination . . . of constituting it elsewhere in fantasy,
where it can freely be without being. This would amount to freeing itself
as pure speech and making us both the fool who can say anything and the
king for whom the words of his fool are of no "consequence."*[29]

At stake here is the necessity to establish precisely how the "other
scene" of the unconscious, of a certain imaginary, of madness, is
discursively constituted, and how the subject is constructed and
situated within this linguistic apparatus.

A technical interpretive point concerning Artaud's writings
might serve our own hermeneutic efforts. In his "Correspondence
with Jacques Rivière" (1924), Artaud, explaining the anomalous
nature of his poetry, writes about the necessity of "the impulse to
think, at each terminal stratification of thought, by means of passing through all the states, all the bifurcations, all the localizations

of thought and of form" (1*:28). While the unconscious conditions of representability might consist of stereotypical images and phrases, the libidinal impulses which mobilize the unconscious within the psychic apparatus are always localized; cathexes always have a referent, even if it is the ego itself. Interpretation cannot escape biographism, referentiality, and representation. Hence the radical historicism and heterogeneity of such a poetics; hence the complexities of any possible notion of poetic causality; hence the seeming formlessness of Artaud's writings.

In itself, we cannot distinguish a "sane" from an "insane" idea or work. Any notion such as *art brut, écrits bruts,* psychopathological art, or *les fous littéraires,* is simultaneously an aesthetic *and* a sociological determination. The pathological or *brut* aspect of such works can only be determined by sociological and psychological considerations, that is, in terms of the material conditions of their creation. Insofar as we are concerned with the influence of such works on modern art, we need mainly consider their formal effects – but we need remember that these works contributed not merely new forms, but also new sensibilities, to modern art. These forms are never dissociated from their accompanying sensibilities: thought exists within the flesh. Artaud writes in "Position of the Flesh" (1925):

There are intellectual screams, screams that come from the delicateness *of the marrow. That is what I call the Flesh. I don't separate my thought from my life. With each vibration of my tongue I retrace all the paths of my thought within my flesh* (1**:51).

For the depths of mental illness reveal the extreme possibilities of the human condition: horrendous psychic pain, radical isolation, total depersonalization, fragmented perceptions, distorted concepts, obsessive activities, theological catastrophes, and mystical bliss of the highest order. Does this reveal an anticultural position, or does it rather disclose the true depths, the dark, suppressed face, of our cultural possibilities?

All that we have said of Artaud's and Novarina's oeuvre, as well as of *écrits bruts,* all that can be selected for translation, reveals only the most superficial, communicable level of such writing. The force of these texts reside, rather, in what cannot be communicated, translated, transliterated, paraphrased, adapted: in the uniqueness of the neologism or the hapax as it inhabits an oeuvre or a language; in the radical disjunctions of agrammatism and malapropism, always grasped within their textual and historical context; in the infinite complexities of a text where a totally disjointed "narrative" reduces discourse to nonsense. Here, perpetual linguist shifts and stresses force us to reconstitute our own lexicon, to recreate our own thought, and to reform our own impossible bodies.

Such considerations border on the theological, heretical and ambiguous as they may be. Nietzsche explains how the breakdown of grammar is intricately related to the death of God; yet at the same time, we find the genesis of a parallel type of linguistic disruption at the rise of a new spirituality, however distanced from the established church it may be. In this regard, Novarina follows in the great Nietzschean tradition of coming to terms with human mortality, by contesting the teleological and eschatological linearity of time. Nietzsche:

"It was" – that is the name of the will's gnashing of teeth and most secret melancholy. . . . The will cannot will backwards; and that he cannot break time and time's covetousness, that is the will's loneliest melancholy. . . . All "it was" is a fragment, a riddle, a dreadful accident – until the creative will says to it, "But thus I willed it."[30]

Nietzsche strives to utilize volition to reverse time and recreate the past, in order to destroy the anxiety of influence and become the unique origin of one's self. The Nietzschean body traversed by the Eternal Return – with its joyous transformation of temporality and its valorization of the creative will – parallels Artaud's pained, scarred "body without organs," which closes itself off to God, time, and eternity, also in a quest to become one's own origin. Both are an attempt to escape metaphysics by means of creative acts which would conquer death and pain; yet one valorizes joy, while the other can never escape suffering. This metaphysical anguish also informs Novarina's project, for he too feels that "time, chronological time, can't be endured! Time is the withering away of things; mechanical time cannot be endured!"

We might end with Novarina's thoughts on the subject, a poetic, antimetaphysical discourse which should further inspire those manipulations of temporality for which the electronic radiophonic medium is especially well suited:

There is something in our chronology, in our temporal references, in our manner of counting time, of naming time, of fragmenting it, that is unbearable. We try to escape it at both ends, to pass beyond it, by making it move backwards, circulating in a circle, by seeking its end, by which one can pass through it. If we were placed within time, it is not in order to endure it, to count it and to remain a prisoner within it, but rather to transpierce it; to occasionally see, in a flash, a time other than that of quotidian successions and boring fictions; and in language, to behold a time other than the schoolish time of subject-verb-complement. To escape, to be saved from mechanical and mortal time by blasts, swoons, ejaculatory bursts and hurled words, by gravitations, and by glimpses of endless swirling. Infinite lists of the repetition of names; perpetual enumeration of numbers: I made all that I can of these techniques in order to emerge from it, to exorcise it. We are people of time, animals sick with time, yet for whom all openings are permitted, through speech. Everybody knows this very well. Man's only passion, his only obsession, is to leave time, by any means: through love, through sport, through ecstasy, through death.[31]

CHAPTER 4

Lost Tongues and Disarticulated Voices:
Gregory Whitehead's *Pressures of the Unspeakable*

The limbo of a nightmare of bones and muscle. – Antonin Artaud

Gregory Whitehead characterizes his radiophonic work as the search for and creation of "the articulate evidence of the disarticulated castaway." This is an oeuvre characterized by elision, fragmentation, degeneration, disintegration, intercuts, cross-references, and multitrack complications. It is a work which recreates radiophonic discourse by means of an extreme, yet highly meditated, linguistic and acoustic violence: the "cut." As such, any attempt to make sense of it would betray it; thus the present study should be read not as synthesis, but rather as a heterogeneous catalog of effects and desires, circuits and short-circuits. The coherence of technology is betrayed by its dangers to our own voices, and to our psychic apparatus. An invasion of our vocal apparatus is ever imminent.

In the introduction to his novel *Crash,* J. G. Ballard proposes the grounds of an apocalyptic contemporary aesthetic: "The marriage of reason and nightmare which has dominated the 20th century has given birth to an ever more ambiguous world. Across the communications landscape move the specters of sinister technologies and the dreams that money can buy."[1] This claim – by the author who insists that the greatest novel of the twentieth century is *Gray's Anatomy* – is schematized in Ballard's equation: "Sex times technology equals the future."[2] The sensual implications of this techno-perversion are spelled out at the very beginning of the novel, where the narrator, speaking of the novel's major protagonist, reveals – well beyond the perversions related in Krafft-Ebing's *Psychopathia Sexualis* and Havelock Ellis's *The Psychology of Sex* – that "Vaughan unfolded for me all his obsessions with the mysterious eroticism of wounds," and continues by admitting that

Vaughan devised a terrifying almanac of imaginary automobile disasters and insane wounds – the lungs of elderly men punctured by door handles, the chests of young women impaled by steering-columns, the cheeks of handsome youths pierced by the chromium latches of quarterlights. For him these wounds were the keys to a new sexuality born from a perverse technology. The images of these wounds hung in the gallery of his mind like exhibits in the museum of a slaughterhouse.[3]

We can find no better introduction to Gregory Whitehead's "Forensic Theater," instantiated by his radio works *Display Wounds* (1986) and *Beyond the Pleasure Principle* (1987). The theme of these perverse "docudramas" is, as the narrator claims, that "no wound ever speaks for itself." The woundscape specialist, the "vulnerologist," must therefore reveal the meaning of wounds and the manner in which the wound serves as a signifier mediating the relationships between the eroticized individual body and the modern technological landscape.

This aesthetic is informed by the peculiarly modernist shocks of trench warfare which had earlier inspired the Italian Futurists, and which provide a "derangement of all the senses" more violent than that dreamed of by Rimbaud or even Lautréamont. Whitehead explains the aesthetic implications of this terror:

Through the accumulation of collective, animal, mechanical, or electronic power into a single blow, the aspiring shock event only truly shocks if it exceeds the capacity of the target individual to absorb external stimuli. A large measure of the resulting sensual derangement centers around the psycho-physical qualities of the look, *both what the shock event looks like as it happens and what the shocked target looks like after.*[4]

[handwritten margin notes: WHAT IT TAKES TO SHOCK / HOW DOES LOOK APPEAR ON RADIO?]

In a metaphysical vein, Gilles Deleuze suggests that "modern painting begins when man no longer sees himself entirely as an essence, but rather as an accident. There is always a fall, the risk of a fall; form proclaims the accident, not the essence."[5] We might eliminate the Aristotelian rhetoric of this paradigm and take this statement literally in order to ask: what are the aesthetic effects of the *physical* accidents that might beset the human figure? The tactical nature of trench warfare in the "Cubist" First World War – that is, the need to look out from the trenches, and the subsequent risk of having one's face blasted away – created a literal deformation, a disfiguration, of the human form, resulting most markedly in the literal loss of face. There ensued the creation of the prosthetic art of radical rhinoplasty (forerunner of cosmetic surgery) – the recreation of destroyed faces. The formal exigencies of these wartime effects were not lost on the history of art, where the aestheticization of war took on the conflicting forms of monumentalization, protest, catharsis. Now, it is the task for such prosthetic creativity to be incorporated into the histories of both aesthetic physiognomy and psycho-linguistics.

The effects of warfare on the art of sound were no less extreme, as is evidenced by the Italian Futurists' fascinations with the technology of war. Consider just one among the many descriptions of the sounds of trench warfare during the First World War, by the Englishman Charles Carrington:

Every gun and every kind of projectile had its own personality. . . . Sometimes a field-gun would leap jubilantly with the job of a Champagne cork from its muzzle, fly over with a steady buzzing crescendo, and burst with a fully expected bang; sometimes a shell would be released from a distant battery of heavies to roll across a huge arc of sky, gathering speed and noise like an approaching express train, ponderous and certain. . . . Some shells whistled, others shrieked, others wobbled through space gurgling like water poured from a decanter.[6]

[handwritten margin notes: but can these sounds be under from their vocals is only sounds different from a Champagne cork bg's]

Such sounds can easily drive a person mad, as is evidenced by the phenomenon of "shell shock." But it is also true that sound can kill:

[handwritten note: SAY MORE ↑ PAPER TOPIC]

apparently a super-whistle driven by a jet engine producing inaudible low tones can destroy human organs by sheer vibration.

Radio is, *a fortiori,* the site of the loss of face and body. Gregory Whitehead's "Forensic Theater" (the generic title of his various related enterprises) is a semiology and libidinal economy of the fractured, fragmented, lost face – as well as of its audiophonic corollary, the shattered, disarticulated voice. This project entails a hermeneutics of the anxious body, always on the verge of being transformed into the memory theater of a morbid anatomy. For wounds constitute the physical manifestations of traumatisms – experiences of shock whose extreme manifestations are amnesia or *aphasia universalis,* a total blockage of conscious expression. As Whitehead explains in his radio work *Display Wounds,* "The theater of wounds is a memory theater. Our failure to look at wounds now, and interpret them now, may lead us to give birth to a society of monsters."[7] Monsters reveal the madness of the imagination, the horrors of the unconscious, the manifestation of alterity and difference in extremis. Though each individual monster is of a formal rarity, monstrosity in general is ubiquitous: monsters symbolize the life of the instincts and the terrors of the soul, regions within the depths of our viscera and beyond the thresholds of rationality, the domain of death itself. It is the grotesque that attunes form with mutation, stasis with transformation, soul with body, life with death.

Sound recording was originally invented to preserve voices beyond the grave in a sort of frozen speech; radio would establish the dissemination of those very same voices.[8] Where once total silence was only possible in death, now the dead continue to speak, sing, make noise, and pollute the body politic, leading to an eerie epistemological rupture. Regarding the shift from music composed in the epoch of a representational episteme to twentieth-century music conditioned by electromechanical repetition and proliferation, Jacques Attali explains:

> *Crisis is no longer a breakdown, a rupture, as in representation, but a decrease in the efficiency of the production of demand, an excess of repetition.* Metaphorically, it is like cancer, while the crisis of representation is like cardiac arrest.[9]

In this simulacral economy, sounds circulate without origin or end, while the age-old metaphorization of the ideal body vanishes in an allegory of pathological mutations. Whitehead's "Forensic Theater" provides an analytic of this electro-pathology. Radio-phonic airspace is a necropolis riddled with dead voices, the voices of the dead, and dead air – all cut off from their originary bodies, all now transmitted to the outer international and cosmic airwaves only in order to reenter our inner ears in a "mad *Totentanz.*"[10] Hence the need to establish a hermeneutic model based on the morbid anatomy of postmortem vocal activity. The "schizophonic" condition of the recorded and broadcast voice is that of the separation of the acoustic event from the lived, eroticized, speaking body. This permits the subsequent dispersal of the disembodied utterance – circulating and decaying on the airwaves, existing beyond the death of the speaking subject. Thanks to recording, our speech has an afterlife, fated to transformation, decay, loss, misprision. Or, as another radio producer-theoretician, Christof Migone, explains, "The static that populates radio air implies a variety of (mis)understandings," irrevocably leading to the recognition that "the disarticulation of the original is not to be regarded as sacrilege, but certainly as transgression. The triad transmission/translation/transgression shares more than a prefix, it implies a common phenomenology: radio."[11] Radiophonic art is guided by the serendipity of a fata morgana, the bewildering, aleatory process of recuperating and rechanneling the lost voice.

Such is the "principia schizophonica." In radiophony, not only is the voice separated from the body, and not only does it return to the speaker as a disembodied presence – it is, furthermore, thrust into the public arena to mix its sonic destiny with that of other voices. Whitehead defines the ontological structure of radio as

a public channel produced by an absent other entering into a private ear. The material specific to radio inscribes itself within the thoroughly unpredictable libidinal circulations internal to a ménage-à-trois. The language of radio is thus constructed not from a series of applied techniques, but from a series of fragile complicities.[12]

We find here the discrete differences between audio art (such as "poésie sonore") and radiophonic art. The material specificity of radiophony relies on: (1) a necessarily electronic mediation; (2) the possible instantaneity of broadcast ("live" radio); (3) the geographic range of transmission, allowing penetration into even the most intimate realms of our private worlds. The true site of radio art is not located in the mere existence of a recorded sound object, but rather in the very manner that this aural fabrication establishes a relationship between an invisible (and perhaps dead!) creator and an equally invisible and usually anonymous (but hopefully living!) listener. The ontological status of this sound object is what Michel Chion writes of as the "acousmètre," referring to a system where sound appears without any corresponding visual correlate – the very feature which permits the radio to be experienced as a spiritual or paranoid receiver, as well as an artistic muse.[13] Whitehead:

> From dissemination, a transmission; from transmission, an interference; from interference, a complicity; and from complicity, the sound of something dripping in the darkest caverns of the cerebral cave.[14]

As in Artaud, the range of inner sounds is as broad as the cosmos, as complex as language, as dense as the viscera and totally unpredictable. Consider Alberto Savinio's short story "Psyche," where the protagonist writes of one character:

> Charles Magne had an uncle in Salonika, a piano tuner and the proprietor of a music shop on Egnazia Street. Charles Magne's uncle was a schizophrenic, and when he was taken to the mental hospital he brandished his tuning fork and shouted out that he wanted to tune the vocal chords of all humanity.[15]

As opposed to the benevolence of Savinio's melomaniacal personage, Whitehead's schizophonica would, quite to the contrary, wish to set all of our voices out of tune, indeed out of body, in a psychoacoustic meltdown or mix-up. It is precisely at the radical limits of radiophony, in its extreme differentiation from the theatrical, musical, poetic, and audio arts, that we can situate the aesthetic practice of Gregory Whitehead – simultaneously a hermeneutic of the morbid disembodied voice and a poetics of schizophonically deteriorating enunciation.

> If radio is to survive inside the play of so many ciphers, the body of the text must reflect in its own composition the aesthetic properties of its environment: the structural multiplicity, the labyrinthine anticipations and interruptions, the sensations of loss and longing, the electro-acoustical comings and goings, the anomalous mix of sensuality and intelligence, of intimacy and objectivity, of frontal physicality and truncated absence.[16]

In the tradition of Marinetti (the celebration of machines, electrical spirits, and orchestras of noise), Welles (extraterrestrial aliens and faked documentaries), Artaud (God replaced by artificial microbes in an electroshocked body without organs), Cage (superimposed tape "mixes" and nonsensical "mesostic" scramblings of words and syllables), and Glenn Gould (polyphonic radio drama instantiated by his "Solitude Trilogy," consisting of *The Idea of the North* [1967], *The Latecomers* [1969], and *The Quiet in the Land* [1977]), Whitehead proffers a new body politic supported by the prosthetic language of the disembody, the antibody, the nobody, the radiobody.[17] However – both inspired by and yet taking issue with Artaud's schizophrenic anti-aesthetic of the "body without organs" – Whitehead suggests that "our Post-Mortem world becomes populated much more significantly by enormous piles of *organs without bodies*."[18] His is a work in which not only will the radiophonic medium be contaminated by disarticulated voices, but in turn speech will be infected by the prosthetic capabilities and shock tactics of the electronic media.[19]

Whitehead cites his particular interest in the possibilities of intersubjective, or rather intercorporeal, exchange through the polemic and practice of innovative recording techniques developed in William Burroughs's *The Ticket That Exploded* (1962):

The realization that something as familiar to you as the movement of your intestines the sound of your breathing the beating of your heart is also alien and hostile does make one feel a bit insecure at first. Remember that you can separate yourself from the "Other Half" from the word. The word is spliced in with the sound of your intestines and breathing with the beating of your heart. The first step is to record the sounds of your body and start splicing them in yourself. Splice in your body sounds with the body sounds of your best friend and see how familiar he gets. Splice your body sounds in with air hammers. Blast jolt vibrate the "Other Half" right out into the street. Splice your body sounds in with anybody or anything. Start a tapeworm club and exchange body sound tapes. Feel right out into your nabor's intestines and help him digest his food. Communication must become total and conscious before we can stop it.[20]

These techniques are at the core of Burroughs's plans to use portable tape recorders to establish a sort of guerilla-media (akin to Situationist techniques), where his cut-up system of textual composition (created in collaboration with Brion Gysin, following Tristan Tzara's dadaist découpage), used in conjunction with the technical possibilities of recording, would operate to create ephemeral street happenings aimed at social critique and direct political action. In "The Electronic Revolution" (1971), Burroughs details the anti-ideological role of such tape works.[21] Arguing that illusion may be

RADIO OR MEANS OF INCORPORATING THE SOUNDS OF ANOTHER

used as a revolutionary weapon, Burroughs suggests that such tapes – with both subliminal and conscious effects – be used to spread rumors, give commands, discredit opponents, scramble and nullify the obsessional associations created by the established media, produce riots. Hidden tape recorders will disseminate phantom voices (previously transmuted by utilizing all of the technical tricks of which the machine is capable), thus subverting the codes of everyday communication and establishing a disquieting, paranoid presence. Such sounds can be projected in numerous manners: individually, in spatially organized grids, or with temporal delays; utilizing loops, audio "flicker", cut-ups and cut-ins of live events to be immediately played back, body sounds, altered political speeches, arbitrary associations of material, variable speed, scrambled language, reverse playback, splicing in of other media (radio and television) broadcasts, audience participation, and so on.

Yet what happens when these socially disruptive techniques of recording technology are interiorized within a poetic system based on specifically radiophonic exigencies?

•∿∿∿• In August 1989, the Australian Broadcasting Company (ABC) program *The Listening Room* aired a documentary produced by Virginia Madsen entitled *Taken by Speed,* dealing with the relations between speed and technology as analyzed in the writings of Paul Virilio. Virilio insists that war requires a logic of accidents, a wisdom derived from the absolute expression of technological risk. In an apparent reversal of Aristotelian logic, he explains that this wisdom is a function of the symmetry between substance and accident. Catastrophe theory becomes not a matter of ruins and effects, but of cinematic and dynamic processes, an exploration of degeneration, decomposition, disintegration, disappearance.[22]

At one point in this radio broadcast, the awe of technology is revealed by children's voices as they explore a hypothetical "Museum of Accidents," described as follows:

Founded 1992. As decreed by the people to have its aim to collect, categorise, define, and to display to the citizens all accidents, disasters, aberrations, mutations, melt-downs, power failures, computer shutdowns, viruses, severed limbs, artificial organs, skipped beats, slipped discs, slips of the tongue, sleights of hand, sunken continents, sunken ships, lost libraries, lost tongues, wreckages of machines, databanks, electronic wiring, accidental discoveries, redundancies, archaisms, space junk, hunks of meteors and asteroids, science fiction writers.[23]

This imaginary museum – displaying an iconology of techno-failure à la J. G. Ballard – could serve (in its sonic manifestations) as a prolegomena to a work also produced by the ABC the year after, Gregory Whitehead's *Pressures of the Unspeakable.*

This piece, a six-week event initiated in October 1991, originated in the fictive "Institute for Screamscape Studies," run by Gregory Whitehead posing as Dr. Scream. The project – presented on Australian radio and television interviews – was to establish the "screamscape" of the "invisible city," that is, to delineate the Sydney nervous system. In a work which, albeit antipodally, puts to the test Artaud's claim in *The Theater and Its Double,* that "nobody in Europe knows how to scream any more" (4:163), listeners would call in to a "scream-line" consisting of a telephone answering machine, in order to have their screams taped and presumedly analyzed.

In addition to framing the nervous system, the telephone-microphone-tape-recorder-radio *circuitry also provided the key for the acoustic demarcation of* pressure in the system: *distortion, the disruption of digital codes, pure unmanageable noise. The scream as an eruption in excess of prescribed circuitries, as capable of "blowing" communications technologies not designed for such extreme and unspeakable meanings.*[24]

Following the accumulation of hundreds of such telephonically gathered screams, the chaotic and disparate material – constituting an archive of screams – was subsequently edited, selected, cut, joined, mixed, and framed in both a pseudo-theoretical narrative and a stereotyped radio-documentary format. A psychoacoustic space was thus created for the screams: "Once given voice, the chorus of screams that drifts through the soundscape of a given region shapes and discloses its identity in condensed and crystallised ways; the screamscape is above all a nervous system, and no two systems feel (or sound) alike."[25] What is certain is that this "nervous system" is simultaneously that of Sydney *and* of Whitehead *and* of radio circuitry – all of which coalesce into a possible alter ego for the moments of our most severe nervous tension. Whitehead substantiates the epistemological conditions of this nearly unendurable "system" with a citation from Wittgenstein: "When you are philosophising, you must descend into primeval chaos and feel at home there."[26] The scream reveals the chaotic depths of linguistic and vocal systems. We may complicate these considerations even further, siding with Artaud and Bataille and parodying Wittgenstein, in claiming, "What cannot be said must result in the outburst of a scream."

The scream may evoke the most profound phantasms as it shatters the coherence of the symbolic. Following the analysis of Guy Rosolato, psychoanalytic theory teaches that "the voice may be defined in the same terms as the Freudian [libidinal] drives. It has a corporeal, organic source of excitation, a force, a field, a pleasurable goal tied to tension that must be reduced, and an object: to reach a receptor and assure communication."[27] The scream represents the extreme manifestation of the voice, a panic sound of stress surpassing the threshold of endurance, signifying the limit of corporeal expression – as opposed to the intellective concerns of thought and the meditative uses of silence. Where the scream communicates, it does so in a uniquely phatic mode of expression, where signification is condensed into the sonic force of the vocal gesture, eschewing all lexical or rhetorical effects.

And yet, in the narrative of *Pressures of the Unspeakable,* the series of "framing" tales by the callers and Whitehead's "analyses" reveal that the psychoacoustic signification of the recorded scream is far from being innocent and unmediated. The "screamscape" lies beyond any possible determination of authenticity. Every scream phoned in is prefaced by an explanation, a brief discourse from the caller explaining the origins, particulars, and sometimes even the style of the scream to come. Furthermore, Dr. Scream interjects his own analyses and typography of screams throughout the work, discussing their totemic and elemental (earth, air, fire, water) classifications, as well as their psychoacoustic shape and verbal power. The very montage of the piece – the ordering of scream evidence, the pseudo-analysis, the canned musical interludes, the mix of dialed-in screams, and Whitehead's own mimicked, faked, "media" screams used as didactic illustrations of the different types – all subvert the documentary credibility of the work's diagnostic theme.[28] Thus, ironically, the *unheimlich* strives towards the *heimlich,* precisely due to the effects of radiophonic mediation.

Yet *Pressures of the Unspeakable* is as much about circuits as it is about screams: the dynamic circuits of libidinal obsession, the closed circuits of corporeal tension, the open circuits of listener feedback, the melodic circuits of the "scream lines." It would be an error to consider *Pressures of the Unspeakable* as merely the sonic object which resulted from the radio event; it is, much more profoundly, a trigger for the release of assorted libidinal energies and the capture of scattered voices. The tape synthesis is but a document of the original acoustic multivoice and multimedia performance.

The implications of the inexorable role of mediation in radiophony were already expressed in a work roughly contemporary with *Pressures . . . ,* Whitehead's *Shake, Rattle, Roll:*

I meant that the whole idea of live radio was an illusion. That the living only speak through the articulated corpses of technology. The dead mediate the living, and so the more dead the transmission, the more alive the sensation. The more dead, the more alive.

These ambiguities are also expressed in his radio work *Lovely Ways to Burn* (1990):

I have put on the table three photographs. One of them is a blowup of the eyes of a woman at a moment of extreme religious ecstasy, a moment of communion with her God, after which she collapsed on the floor in a trance, and began to speak in tongues. The second photograph, okay, going from the sacred to the profane, is the eyes, again, just a blowup of the eyes, of an individual at a moment of erotic ecstasy. And finally I have blown up just the eyes, isolated the eyes, on the face of an individual who has just been subjected to a rather severe voltage of electroshock therapy. . . . And now you tell me if you can tell the difference.

In this mental experiment mimicking that of the famous cinematic montage experiments of the early Russian filmmaker Kuleshov – where the meaning of a face's expression was determined by the differing narrative contexts in which the identical close-up of a single face was alternatively spliced – Whitehead's description satisfies the sundry iconographic requirements of theology, eroticism, and technology.

On 16 June 1875 the trial of the photographer Jean Buguet took place in Paris. Buguet specialized in the phenomenon of "spiritualist" photography, that is, seances in which a client's portrait was taken, so that the background mysteriously revealed the image of a beloved deceased person. The procedure was simple: the customer was questioned about the physical characteristics of the dead person; a photograph of the client was taken; later, in the darkroom, the image of a headless puppet covered in a mysterious shroud, crowned by the photo of a face resembling the deceased, was superimposed on the background of the client's photograph. The physiognomy of the deceased was matched with its spirit-image by choosing from an extensive photographic file organized according to facial types, a prefiguration of more scientific classifications to come. In the 1880s, under the influence of the theories of Lombroso, the criminological procedures of Alphonse Berthillon established a statistically based filing system in which photographic portraiture and anthropometric description were combined into an identificatory scheme. Before the fact, Buguet created a corrupted version of this system in order to produce simulacra of the dead. Despite testimony from many satisfied customers, the system broke down one day when a man arrived, wishing to be photographed with his recently deceased young bride – the following day he received his own image alongside that of the bearded visage of a fireman!

The phantasms behind the origins of sound recording were not very different. Edison patented the phonograph in 1877, the same year that Charles Cros invented a similar device in France. Edison's initial motivation was to preserve, and not replicate or transmit, sound. More specifically, he wrote:

We will be able to preserve and hear again, one year or one century later, a memorable speech, a worthy tribune, a famous singer, etc. . . . We could use it in a more private manner: to preserve religiously the last words of a dying man, the voice of one who has died, of a distant parent, a lover, a mistress.[29]

Sound fidelity was to help heal the wounds of nostalgia, and to prolong the more fickle emotional fidelity of love – signified in the very timbre of the human voice, and now made available to an ever-fading memory.

Gregory Whitehead's radiophonic art exists, *a fortiori*, under the sign of *prosopopoeia*, which,

consists in somehow staging absent people, the dead, supernatural beings, and even inanimate objects; in making them act, speak, and respond, as well as being heard; or at least in taking them as confidants, witnesses, respondants, accusors, avengers, judges, etc.; and all that, whether feigned or seriously, according to whether or not one is the master of one's own imagination.[30]

As such, prosopopoeia is the rhetorical figure which manifests the hallucinatory, paranoid, supernatural, or schizophrenic presence of invisible, deceased, ghoulish, demonic, or divine others. Whitehead accomplishes these conditions of vocal disembodiment not only through the utilization of audiophonic *truquage* (special effects), but also by a taped and electronically inspired rethinking and revitalization of classical rhetorical tropes and figures. As his iconography is guided by the disarticulation and decay of the body, so is his poetics established according to the accumulation, combination, permutation, and substitution of linguistic elements. All of these linguistic "aberrations" – especially glossolalia, dissonance, cacophony, invention of pseudo-language, expansion of vocal timbre – are inflected or "infected" by electronically recorded or produced sounds. Thus traditional rhythmic patterns of locution, modulated by corporeal processes (breathing, heartbeat, blood circulation, nervous system humming) as well as by interruptions of locution (coughing, sneezing, wheezing, gagging, hiccups, borborygmus) are all subject to transformation, highlighting, or suppression by means of the cutting knife of tape montage.

Every author, every style, every artistic movement, and indeed every theoretical position, favors a more or less limited range of rhetorical forms. (Consider, for example, the central role of metaphor and metonymy in Surrealist aesthetics, following the Freudian metapsychological analysis of condensation and displacement in the dreamwork, augmented by Lacanian structural considerations.) The classic rhetorical treatment at the lexical, syntactic, and textual level obtains in Whitehead's work, augmented by new tape capabilities – cutting, montage, mixing – which permit treatment at the syllabic, phonemic, and morphemic level. The categories of such rhetorical operations may be broadly construed in the arithmetic terms of addition, subtraction, multiplication, division.[31] As such, some of the major terms that may be used to describe Whitehead's key rhetorical ploys would be: *antisthecon* (substituting a letter or sound for another within a word), *epenthesis* (addition of a letter, sound, or syllable to the middle of a word), *metaplasm* (moving letters or syllables from their natural places), *metathesis* (transposition of the order of letters or syllables in a word), *syntagmatic amalgam* (expressing several assertions in a single word by utilizing elisions and new juxtapositions), *prosthesis* (addition of a letter or syllable to the beginning of a word), *paragoge* (adding a letter or syllable to the end of a word), *aposiopesis* (a sudden interruption), *brachylogy* (excessive brevity), *ellipsis* (suppression of words), *erosion* (repetition in which, at each return, a part of the word or text disappears), *syncope* (the removal of a letter or syllable from the middle of a word), *systole* (shortening a vowel or syllable), *palindrome* (a phrase offering the same meaning read in either direction), *barbarism* (the use of foreign elements), *tmesis* (the division of a word by the intercalation of one or several words), and *anacoluthon* (a syntactical rupture).

Examination of the transcript of one of Whitehead's radio works, *How to Pronounce "Prosthesis"* (1991), will illustrate many of these rhetorical issues:

How to Pronounce "Prosthesis"
(read slowly, in a canned voice)

i, a, m, t, he, p, ro-s, t-he, s, i, s
a, m, t, he pro s, the s i si
m, t, he, p rost, he-s, is i a
t he p rost he, s is i, a,m
he pro-s, thesis, i am t

e pro-s, the sis, i am t h
pro-s, the s-i-s, i, a, m, the
rost he, sisiam, t he, p
o s, the sisi a m, t hepr
s the sisi a, m the p-ro

the sisi am, t, he pros
he s, i, si amt heprost
e sisi amt he prosth
isi amt he pros the
siam the prosthesi

i am the prosthesis
i am the prosthesis
i am the prosthesis

how would you like to go through life
hearing nothing more than that?

This work – appearing on the page like concrete poetry or sound poetry – reveals the ongoing thematic of the audiophonic prosthetic phantasm, without, however, instantiating all of its possibilities. It remains a formalist language play amenable to purely vocal recitation, as do several of Whitehead's other works, such as *Ciao/ ouch* – a palindrome where the recitation of the two words (and their derivatives "ich," "itch," "asch") is cut up at the syllabic and morphemic level, and then redistributed as babble – might be considered an extreme condensation signifying the nostalgic wounds of departure, in the tradition of Apollinaire's miniature poem consisting simply of the words "Luth / Zut!" *Oral or Anal?* (1988) consists of the uncut vocal recitation of permutations of the syllables in the title, organized by a slippage where one letter is rotated with each reading, for example: "LORA LO RANA ALOR AL ORAN." Does *Oral or Anal?* pose a question about sexuality, about the eroticism of a normal body *with* organs? Is it an exclusive or inclusive disjunction, imposing a sexual injunction? Or does it rather bespeak the manifest impossibility (but distinct, if perverse, radiophonic possibility) of *organs without a body!?* In any case, this category of Whitehead's works – though composed and produced for radio broadcast – does not, strictly speaking, surpass the limits of audio art, as does *Pressures of the Unspeakable.* But these works do, in fact, allegorize the corporeal "cuts" and "mix" which define radical radiophony.

Poetry is, as Paul Valéry claimed, "a prolonged hesitation between sound and sense."[32] Hence the discordance between metric and linguistic structures that obtains in the scansion and recitation of poetic texts. As psycholinguist Ivan Fónagy explains, the hesitation, vacillation, equivocation, and indetermination entailed in choosing between the disarticulation of syntax in order to maintain a coherent metrics and the destruction of musicality in order to respect the signification and logic of the enunciation.[33] In the recitation of poetry, the obedience to poetic and theatrical laws – a musicality which depends upon the regularity of the distribution of fundamental frequencies in each syllable, and which therefore depends upon the relative eschewal of noise – results in an enrichment of the message. For example, an actor from Stanislavski's theater in Moscow recounts that during his audition he was asked to draw forty different meanings from the phrase "This evening."[34]

Thus there is yet another poetic mode beyond the limits of musication, where "noises – the expressive distortion of neutral articulations, the displacement of accents, unexpected pauses, absence of grammatical pauses – is transformed into a message."[35] Essentially, many noises constitute hapax legomena. The very possibility of language's flexibility, and of poetry per se, is constituted by the distortion, inflection, degradation, disarticulation, impairment, corruption, pollution, contamination, decomposition, erosion, lesion, abrasion, fracture, rupture, mutilation, wreck, or ruin of language. Indeed, an indefinite but vast number of predicates is necessary to describe the parasitic effects of noise, as each noise creates a different effect within the linguistic system, at both the level of language and speech. Furthermore, we should remember the random structural complexity of noise in relation to musical sounds, which makes noise considerably more difficult to grasp and enjoy than more structured sounds, such as those of music, poetry, or even everyday speech.

Flexibit, make noise hard to understand/ enjoy ⊃ destabilizing.?

Following the above considerations of the sound structure of poetry, a parallel analysis obtains for the relations between noise and music. In his book *Noise,* Jacques Attali explains that music "has the explicit function of *reassuring:* the whole of traditional musicology analyzes music as the organization of controlled panic, the transformation of anxiety into joy, and of dissonance into harmony."[36] Every system bears within itself the origins of its own destruction; in music, it is noise that establishes a process of rupture in the musical system by creating a catastrophe point beyond which resolution is no longer possible. Noise creates new meaning both by interrupting the old meanings *and* by consequently unchanneling auditory perception and thus freeing the imagination. (This liberation of sound and audition was precisely the goal of John Cage's celebration of the role of noise in music.) "It makes possible the creation of a new order on another level of organization, of a new code in another network."[37] What is of particular interest in our analysis is that "even when a new technology is an external noise conceived as a reinforcement for a code, a mutation in its distribution often profoundly transforms the code."[38]

The work of Gregory Whitehead constitutes, mutatis mutandis, just such a mutation of the system of audiophonic/radiophonic codes, precisely by being attuned to the fragility of the human vocal apparatus and the morbid body. Whitehead not only utilizes the extreme yet traditional theatrical and musical malleability of his own, untampered voice to create numerous dramatic personages, alter egos, and songs. More notably, he dismembers his taped virtuosic voice, transforms it into noise, and inserts it into the radiophonic apparatus – subsequently interiorizing the exigencies of that very same apparatus in his own imagination and symbolic system.

A case in point would be Whitehead's *Principia Schizophonica* (1991), where a discursive lecture on the radio disembody is interrupted at the syllabic level, at an ever increasing frequency, by diverse noises which are spliced in, including fragments from other of Whitehead's previous works. Not only does Whitehead cut up the voice; he furthermore splices voices into the cuts. Here, the sonorous value of noise is equal to that of meaningful sentences; yet paradoxically, the referent of the discourse itself is in fact the very noise which is interrupting it. Also instantiating these issues is *O Solo Mio* (1988), a "degeneration" piece which departs from the realm of rigorous formalism, insofar as each repetition of the chanted opening bars of this tune loses an increasing number of syllables, as the words are replaced by noises – found sounds that Whitehead terms "guttural linguistic garbage," "dirt," "wounds" – which are spliced into the song. *O Solo Mio* pushes formalism into a new domain, well *beneath* the meaningful level of poetic sense. Even further, the intimate relations between voice and tape are revealed in *Eva, can I stab bats in a cave?* (1985), where the palindrome is recorded, played backwards, performed backwards in viva voce, rerecorded, and finally played backwards – to end up with a twisted "forward" simulacrum. This procedure – instantiating the trope of *hysteron-proteron,* that is, reading backwards – speaks to the age-old phantasy of arresting and reversing the passage of time. For, if one can read backwards, one can recede to the origin, and begin again. The ill will, the ressentiment, against the ravages of time may be abolished as temporality itself becomes totally malleable. Nietzsche's phantasm of the Eternal Return, and Novarina's desire to escape temporal inexorability, is finally manifested by the empirical means of tape erasure, reversal, and playback. Time is marked, cut, and redeployed.

Formalism and performance cedes to "diagnostic" in a series of works, exemplified by *If a voice like, then what?,* which articulates such a confusion of tongues, a mix of vocal and electronic elements which defies imitation. In this work we are asked, "Do you have a voice like . . . ? followed by composite recorded sounds which couldn't possibly exist as a human enunciation. Each of these sounds actually consists of numerous recorded samplings of Whitehead's own voice, both spoken normally and distorted through megaphones, then cut up, fragmented, damaged, and finally sutured through four-track mixing. Might we presume that this voice exists in the subjunctive mood of radiophony, a sound that is never truly heard? Such elocutionary monsters exist both within the recorded voice *and* in the realm of the putative ideal listener, who is assured at the end of the piece that modern medical techniques can indeed "correct" such speech impediments.

Guided by the trope of the *logatom* – an invented word deprived of meaning, utilized in tests of auditory perception and memory – Whitehead's "speech tests" and "correctives," with their mix of found and recorded sound, word and noise, sense and nonsense, provide a concerted critique of the utilitarian value of rhetorical analysis, the theatrically oriented poetics of contemporary radio, the efficacy of representation, and the very problematic of the originality of the avant-garde. These considerations are also manifested in *The Problem with Bodies* (1988), where we are asked to repeat the proposition "The problem with bodies is the reason for antibodies, and the problem with antibodies is no body at all," first without using our tongues, then without opening our mouths, and finally without using our larynx. We might indeed say that the problem with bodies cannot truly be expressed, since the body is neither purely natural nor purely textual, but rather the primal symbolic system which articulates nature and culture. As transformed by the rerecording, looping, and feedback capabilities of sound engineering (especially given the sub-liminal, micro-phonic levels of digital sampling), the human voice in radiophonic art will project the voice of "nobody," which, like Artaud's "body without organs," is proposed as an antidote to the ills that beset the fragile, tortured body in pain.

We must therefore rethink the radio in terms of another articulatory – or rather disarticulatory – site of the symbolic, not representing the body but rather *transforming* or *annihilating* it. The phantasm of a body without organs radically disrupts the very forms of our discourse. The same might be said for the phantasm of a body-with-too-many-organs, or a deformed body with hypertrophied or hypotrophied organs, or organs-without-a-body. Such a Rabelaisian or Nietzschean body might incite a confusion of tongues to match the intracorporeal battle – the antagonism or agony – of organs and muscle groups which can only culminate in silence or a scream.

POSTFACE

. . . soi, quoi, loi, moi, roi, toi, zut et Ça . . . – Antonin Artaud

In 1874, indignant about the failure of his play *La révolte,* Villiers de l'Isle-Adam wrote one of his *Contes cruels* (*Cruel Tales*), entitled "La machine à gloire" ("The Glory Machine"), dedicated to his friend Stéphane Mallarmé. This story is one of his sardonic diatribes against the progress of modernity; ironically, it presents what may be deemed the ultimate manifestation of the theater of cruelty. As Artaud's work instantiates and incarnates his life, his veritable theater of cruelty is a theater of one and for one. Conversely, Villiers' theatrical machine is a theater of cruelty within which we all, as spectators, enter the scenario, where the play itself is no longer necessary to create an aesthetic effect. Villiers suggests that in the theater, the *claque*, the hired clappers, are a deception necessary to the success, indeed to the very existence, of the production. Furthermore, the *claque* is itself an artform, manifesting the entire gamut of expressivity. Beyond the varied types of clapping, there are also a myriad of vocal effects: the initial, basic *bravo*, is soon transformed into *brao;* one then passes on to the paroxysmic *Oua-Ouaou*, which finally evolves into the definitive scream, *Brâ-oua-ouaou,* nearly a bark. But, in fact, these are still only the most basic effects; there is an entire range of special effects of which the *claque* is capable – not unlike those theatrical efforts of Artaud's theater of cruelty:

> *Will we ever finish with this if we wish to examine all the resources of a well organized* claque? – *Let us mention, nevertheless, in regard to those "spicy" pieces and emotional dramas, the Screams of frightened women, choked Sobs, truly communicative Tears, little brusque Laughs . . . the Clicking of snuff boxes in whose generous depths the emotionally moved man has recourse, Howls, Chokings, Encore!, Recalls, silent Tears, Threats, Recalls with additional Howls, Pounding of approbation, uttered Opinions, Wreaths, Principles, Convictions, moral Tendencies, epileptic Attacks, Childbirth, Insults, Suicides, Noises of discussions (Art-for-art's-sake, Form and Idea), etc., etc.*[1]

The final word of this art is when the *claque* itself shouts, "Down with the *claque!*" and then applauds the piece as if they were the real public. As Villiers explains, "The *claque* is to dramatic glory what Mourners are to Suffering."

   Even so, this is but mere art; Villiers suggests the possibility of eliminating the aleatory effects of the *claque* by mechanizing the process to avoid all chance effects, thus absolutely guaranteeing the play's success. This is the "Glory Machine," which will be constituted by the theater auditorium itself, where the entire audience will surreptitiously be transformed into the *claque.* In this apparatus, the sound effects are perfected by multiplying the presence of gilded angels and caryatids, whose mouths bear phonographic speakers to emit the appropriate sounds at critical moments; the pipes that supply the lamps with gas are augmented by others to introduce laughing gas and tear gas into the auditorium; the balconies are equipped with mechanisms to hurl bouquets and wreaths onstage; spring-operated canes are hidden in the feet of the chairs, so as to reinforce the ovations with their striking. In fact, the apparatus is so powerful that it can, literally, bring down the house, such that the theater would be totally destroyed!

In this masterpiece of ressentiment, Villiers manages to eradicate the need for actor, scenario, and scene. Everything is reduced to audience reaction, in what is not quite a conceptual theater, but rather a purely sensual stagecraft, open to all possible spectators. The event consists of the immediate inscription of effects on the spectator's body – a technique of theaterless theater which will be perfected by the drug culture of the 1960s. Artaud's theater of cruelty, though no less "cruel," bears certain resemblances to Villier's, but has quite different effects. In its radical biographism and psychologism, it is a theater for one alone. For Artaud, the body is the microcosm of the theater, a corporeal stage and auditorium. Ultimately, stage, script, *and* audience are eliminated; the entire drama takes place within Artaud's soul and within his writings. But this is less ironic and less paradoxical than one might at first surmise, for the coalescing of actor and spectator within this impossible theater coincides with the diffracted condition of schizophrenic thought: split between multiple identities, this "other scene" is one in where the individual plays all roles, being simultaneously subject and spectator, as if watching from without – as in dreams or in the primal scene. "There are imbeciles who believe themselves to be beings, beings by innateness. As for me, I must flog my innateness in order to exist" (1*:9). To read Artaud's writing is to be flogged by it; but what proof of our own inner being will this punishment reveal? How will we perceive our own totems, our own gods?

In his first book, *Le Schizo et les langues* (*The Schizo and Languages*), Louis Wolfson – who variably describes himself as "the student of schizophrenic languages," "the mentally ill student," "the student of insane idioms" – provides a "mad" linguistic theory to explain his unique relation to English, his mother tongue.[2] The book consists of autobiographical fragments interspersed with, indeed interrupted by, phonetic analyses of his new use of language. Wolfson (who wrote the book in French at the age of thirty-nine, while living in New York City), during several incarcerations in psychiatric hospitals, was diagnosed as an obsessive, paranoid schizophrenic. Not able to bear his mother's voice, and by extension, the sound of his "mother tongue," Wolfson utilized several strategies for escaping from this painful idiom: plugging his ears with his fingers; plugging one ear with a finger and the other with a radio earplug; wearing double radio earplugs, and later Walkman head-phones. These varied "deafeners" functioned by either blocking out sound or by replacing the hated sounds of the English language with foreign language programs and music. His entire life was lived to the background of constant radio chatter.

But all of these were merely passive defenses: when caught unaware, he would simply scream at the top of his voice to drown out the horrendous English language. Yet his masterstroke was the active, immediate, spontaneous transformation of English into its panglossic double. He accomplished this by studying several languages (French, German, Russian, Hebrew), with the intent of utilizing them in varied combinations to dissimulate English. He would achieve this transformation word by word, by means of finding a homophonic synonym in another language, such as the German *Milch* or the Danish *mælk* for the English *milk*. For more complicated terms, he would disarticulate the word and provide syllabic substitutions culled from different languages, for example: in the term *vegetable shortening, vegetable* is easily transformed into the French *végétal;* for *shortening,* the first syllable /sh/ is broken up into the Hebrew *chemenn* (grease) and the German *Schmalz* (grease), the syllable /or/ is transformed into the Russian *jir,* and the suffix *ing* becomes the German *ung.* Or he would invent neologisms, such as the substitution of *urlich* for *early.*

To escape the torments of a living language, Wolfson retires to the dead language of dictionaries, letting lexical coincidences rule his discourse. Yet here is the paradox, and the irony, of his situation: his linguistic method is circular, since the homophonic substitutions only transform the hated English into something sounding like English – but with a totally idiosyncratic, very heavy, polyglot accent! He traverses the languages of the world in order to return to the suppressed English idiom, just as his perpetual attempts to escape from his mother's voice would eventually lead him, in his second book, to reflect upon his profound bond to it, and to her. Nevertheless, it must be noted that the very possibility of such linguistic studies was effected by the passive defense mechanism of listening to the radio, which drowned out his mother's voice, as well as all other traces of English (a difficult task indeed in the city of New York). This use of language is not communicative, but rather a move toward psychic isolation.

Perhaps the most poignant exception to this solitude (which coincided with an almost total sexual dysfunction) is related in the following incident. Playing instrumental music quite loudly on a powerful portable radio in the streets, he loved to

impose, as it were, this music on the passersby as if he were serenading them, as if perhaps he, and not the radio, made the music; and any theme, any motif, any phrase, any measures, truly seemed to him so much better if a pretty girl listened to these sounds while passing.[3]

This failed attempt at "radiophonic" communication and seduction, this radio serenade, is not unlike the current public posturing with "boom boxes": a mode of social interaction, self-identity, and allurement which is the antithesis of the nearly solipsistic pleasure and unity created by the Walkman craze.

Failed seduction? but is claiming space

Wolfson's second book, *Ma mère, musicienne, est morte . . .*, also written in French, bears as its full title: *Ma mère, musicienne, est morte de maladie maligne mardi à minuit au milieu du mois de mai mille977 au mouroir Memorial à Manhattan* (*My Mother, Musician, Died of a Malignant Illness on Tuesday at Midnight in the Month of May One Thousand977 in Memorial Mortuary in Manhattan*). His mother, who died a terrible death of cancer, kept a detailed diary of her illness, from which selections are translated and added to Wolfson's own literary account of her death. He explains, "My book has a double title and two authors: *Ma mère, musicienne, est morte . . .* or *Exterminez l'Amérique,* by Rose Minarsky & Louis Wolfson." While in *Le Schizo et les langues* Wolfson accentuated all that was necessary to separate himself from his mother, in *Ma mère, musicienne, est morte . . .* he strives towards an ultimate reconciliation and attachment, to the extent that at one point he even makes a syntactic error entailing the confusion of himself and his mother: "Tuesday, during the day, my mother complained me [*se me plaignait*] a couple of times about feeling an abdominal pain upon getting off of the bus."[4] Both the curious construction *se me plaignait* and the unidiomatic use of *une couple* express his newfound attachment to, and identification with, his mother. He goes even further, for in hearing that his mother's cancer began in her ovaries, Wolfson exclaims, "I vaguely thought that I too equally began, so to speak, in the ovary."[5] He identifies with his mother, with her pain, her disease, her death.

It is precisely the conditions of her death that brought mother and son together through a series of ironies. Now it is the mother who is confined to the hospital, as the son was previously incarcerated in psychiatric institutions; now the earphones of his Walkman become like stethoscopes; now his music, no longer needed as a defense against his mother, triumphs, while her singing voice and organ playing are stilled. Louis Wolfson and his mother, as well as their two texts, are joined by death, which equalizes everything in silence. The rewritten, definitive version of *Le Schizo et les langues,* was rebaptised *Point finale à une planète infernale* [*The End of an Infernal Planet*]. This retitling, along with the apocalyptic pronouncements in *Ma mère, musicienne, est morte . . .* , are his means of coming to terms with human suffering and the incomprehensibility of death. Bewailing the ills of the world, he sees the only possible cure in a total radioactive sterilization of the planet, a "planetary euthanasia," a "super-colossal collective Bang!" He cites the Bible in explanation: "There shall be an end to death, and to mourning and crying and pain; for the old order has passed away!" (*Apocalypse,* 21:4).[6] It is theorized that the "big bang" which created the universe spewed out powerful radio waves, thus constituting the primal radio broadcast. For Wolfson, the universe was to end in the same manner, since nuclear explosions also create a tremendous output of radio waves: universal history, from archē to telos, exists from radio blast to radio blast, mediated in Wolfson's prophetic case by a psychic apparatus perpetually soothed by radio babble. The book ends:

I obviously do not know how many millions, billions, nonillions (is this even a finite number?) of planets suffered a true nuclear euthanasia that night of 17 and 18 May 1977, but, quite unfortunately, the Earth was not (yet?) among them![7]

His internalized, defensive, paranoid use of broadcast music and talk as an isolation mechanism (*Le schizo et les langues*) has been exteriorized and aggrandized, giving way to the even more paranoid desire for an apocalyptic cataclysm, to be followed by the infinite silence of universal death. Has a more touching eulogy ever been written?

In two recent radio works, *A Hole in the Head* (National Public Radio, 1993) and *The Transpiring Transistor Series* (EARS, Banff Center for the Arts, 1992), Christof Migone produced audio versions of several texts of *écrits bruts,* inspired by the following writers: Aloïse Corbaz, Jules Doudin, Émile Josome Hodinos, Jacqueline, Marmor, Sylvain Lecoq, and others.[8] As Migone explains in a text devoted to this project, the radiophonic valorization of such radical individuality in the face of institutions establishes a situation where *bruts* are transformed into *bruits,* into noise. This led him to theorize the radio artist as a "transpiring transistor," whose subversive function is described as follows: "It performs a kind of reading/listening that is inseparable from writing/voicing. In its desire for a herniated body of text, it utilizes all senses to ferret its subjects."[9] Here is the paradox: when the "subject" ferreted out is the author of the radio text, the circuit is solipsistic; when the subject sought is a listener – especially in "live" talk radio, with the requisite listener feedback – the active voice of radio is enacted.

Migone explains the condition of the first part of the paradox with a modernist, experimental twist on Berkeley's conundrum about whether the sound of a tree falling in a forest with nobody to hear it actually exists: "Radio, here, refers to an action rather than an instrument; radio as a particular manifestation of the act: to radiate. Radio is the loop of a collapsing tree, endlessly emanating static. Whether someone listens is inconsequential to the transmitter."[10] The solipsistic radiophonic transmitter – connected in metaphysical parallel to the equally solipsistic writers of *écrits bruts* – exists within the fearful void of the universe, for such is the infinite space of radio.

There's no language of radio, just tongues. It's a vocabulary afloat and unanchored, enamoured with possibilities. . . . With regard to the Bruts *writings I hear these texts, and cannot help (nor do I want to) as a novice* transpiring transistor *finding a simultaneous series of cacaphonous* [sic] *stammers, sentences and screeches emanating from my mouth.*[11]

Louis Wolfson utilizes the radio primarily as a barrier to protect himself from the hated mother tongue: radio sound becomes a substitute for those screams which could also, but with more effort and less pleasure, effect the same goal. Christof Migone, to the contrary, begins with *écrits bruts,* hoping to discover or invent that sort of radio static which could protect him from the media institution, to subvert it from within. Both are manners of short-circuiting the communicative apparatus. Are these two procedures not, somehow, inverted parts of the same project: poetic, radiophonic, cosmic?

But what happens when the circuit is complete? What then is the relation between radio person and radio persona? Can the two ever be differentiated? Might radio utopia be precisely the confluence of the two? In one of Christof Migone's radio productions, *Describe Yourself* (from a live on-air show for the Montreal community station CKUT, 1991), listeners were requested to telephone the station and do precisely what the title suggests. This sort of work constitutes a paradigm of the second half of the paradox of radio. The response of one of the callers might well serve as a biographical portrait of the perfectly schizophonic radio artist, or perhaps also of a particularly astute schizophrenic:

CALLER 6: *I would describe myself as subterranean, obscure, black, poetic, infrequent, defossilized, primary, unfulfilled, desiring, funny, frantic, myopic, skinless, untouchable, paralogic, incompetent, silent, freaked out, unfamiliar, dry, speckless, insincere, crazy, wanton, lustful, and completely selfless.*

"Completely selfless?" But of course: every radio personality is self-less, once the self is broadcast. In any case, can we know whether this is the voice of another person, or just another persona of Migone? This uncertainty principle is the central aporia of travel on the airwaves.

•*MWV*• Villiers's antitheater, Artaud's theater of cruelty, Cage's imaginary landscapes, Novarina's theater of the ears, Wolfson's radio solipsism, Whitehead's forensic theater, Migone's radio contortionism: can the heterotopia of radically experimental radiophony lead to a linguistic utopia, or are its results necessarily dystopic? I wish to end this study with one further selection from *Describe Yourself,* which might serve as a coda, perhaps even an allegory, and certainly a warning:

CALLER 7: *The wires. Hello.*
H: *Yes. What is your shape?*
C7: *The wires. The wires for the electricity. It's the power. The wires. You know what I mean?*
H: *Yeah.*
C7: *When I stand near the wires and the tower of the powers.*
H: *What does that have to do with you?*
C7: *Interesting things. Short circuit feedback.*

Here, loss of self paradoxically entails the most weighty presence of selfhood and self-consciousness. Indeed, the precondition of the "wireless" apparatus is precisely the wires, the dynamo, the power, the institution – reason enough to be paranoid. Is this an expression of anxiety and fear? Or is it rather the case, as Migone suggests, that radiophony "is a pleasure grounded in the insecurity of its ground, a certain danger in the paradise of unbalanced inputs and dizzy spells."[12] The electrical metaphor is unavoidable; the "ground" exists to connect the radiophonic apparatus to the earth, precisely so that it may be sublimated into the ether of interstellar space.

Yet there is a simpler, more commonplace risk to the radiophonic arts: we must never forget that when the switch is turned off, all that is left are the inaudible vibrations of an infinitude of radio waves – and the human voice.

HOW DOES THIS SEPARATION OCCUR

NOTES

PREFACE

1 See also Allen S. Weiss, "Broken Voices, Lost Bodies: Experimental Radio-phony," in *Perverse Desire and the Ambiguous Icon* (Albany: State University of New York Press, 1994).

2 Though there is no comprehensive history of radio, experimental or other-wise, the most useful sources to date are Douglas Kahn and Gregory Whitehead, eds., *Wireless Imagination: Sound, Radio, and the Avant-Garde* (Cambridge: MIT Press, 1992); Neil Strauss, ed., *Radiotext(e),* a special issue of *Semiotext(e),* no. 16 (1993); Daina Augaitis and Dan Lander, eds., *Radio Rethink: Art, Sound and Transmission* (Banff: Walter Phillips Gallery, 1994).

3 Geert Lovink, "The Theory of Mixing: An Inventory of Free Radio Techniques in Amsterdam," in *Mediamatic* 6, no. 4 (1992): 225.

4 The prehistory of radio and audio art is traced out in a detailed chronology established by Hugh Davis, "A History of Recorded Sound," in Henri Chopin, *Poésie sonore internationale* (Paris: Jean-Michel Place, 1979), pp. 13–40.

5 See Friedrich Kittler, *Discourse Networks, 1800–1900* (1985), translated from German by Michael Metteer with Chris Cullens (Stanford: Stanford University Press, 1990), pp. 177–264, passim.

6 See the catalog of the exhibition *Junggesellenmaschinen/Les machines célibataires,* inspired by the work of Michel Carrouges, and edited by Harald Szeemann (Venice: Alfieri, 1976).

7 Lewis Tom, *Empire of the Air* (New York: HarperCollins, 1991), pp. 73–77.

8 Farabet's comments were set forth in a seminar on montage theory directed by Jacques Munier at the Collège International de Philosophie, in Paris, during the session of June 1992.

I. FROM SCHIZOPHRENIA TO SCHIZOPHONICA

1 Anaïs Nin, *The Diary, 1931–1934* (New York: The Swallow Press and Harcourt Brace & World, 1966), pp. 191–92. The narrative position from the point of view of the dead is utilized in several modern texts such as William Faulkner, *As I Lay Dying;* Claude Lanzmann, *Shoah;* and Edgar Allan Poe, "The Facts in the Case of M. Valdemar."

2 Susan Sontag, *Illness as Metaphor* (New York: Vintage, 1979).

3 *Pour en finir avec le jugement de dieu* appears in Antonin Artaud, *Oeuvres complètes* (Paris: Gallimard, 1974), vol. 13; all references to Artaud's *Oeuvres complètes* will be cited in parentheses, with the volume number followed by the page number in Arabic numerals. Vols. 1 and 14 were each published in two separate parts, indicated by one or two asterisks. All translations are my own, unless otherwise stated.

4 Other versions of this work, and further renunciations of his Christianity, include "Lettre ouverte à Pie XII" (22:381); "Adresse au Pape" (23:155–58); (23:410–11); (23:451–53); (23:454–55). See also "L'Evêque de Rodez" (9:217–22).

5 Cited in notes to Artaud, *Oeuvres complètes,* vol. 1, p. 241.

6 On the linguistic and theological aspects of the *Cahiers de Rodez,* see Allen S. Weiss, "Psychopompomania," *A+T* [*Art & Text*] 27 (1977); reprinted in Allen S. Weiss, *The Aesthetics of Excess* (Albany: State University of New York Press, 1989).

7 On glossolalia, see the works cited in footnote 5 of Allen S. Weiss, "Psychopompomania." See also the two issues of *Le Discours Psychoanalytique* 6 and 7 (March and June 1983), edited by Jean-Jacques Courtine; and the issue of *Langages* 91 (1988), also edited by Courtine. Gilles Deleuze, in *Logique du sens* (Paris: Minuit, 1969), offers an important comparison of Artaud and Lewis Carroll, in the chapter entitled "Du schizophrène et de la petite

fille," pp. 101–14. Despite the radical differences between the glossolalia and "nonsense" texts of children, poets, and schizophrenics, it is of interest at least to note the structural similarities. Clayton Eshelman's translation is published in Douglas Kahn and Gregory Whitehead, eds., *Wireless Imagination* (Cambridge: MIT Press, 1992), pp. 309–29.

8 Artaud's pronunciation of his glossolalia (whose written phonetic structure borrowed from Turkish and Greek, his mother's "mother tongue") was not quite French, as Paule Thévenin explains in a note to *Artaud le mômo:* for the most part his pronunciation was closer to the Italian than to the French. For example, the *e* is never mute; *u* is pronounced *ou; z* is pronounced *dz; g* is always hard, and slightly guttural when followed by *h;* the final *ch* is pronounced somewhat like the German *ch* (12:267). These transformations of the French language become pertinent and distinctive features of Artaud's written and spoken texts, thus a highly marked feature of his theatrical (and not only psychopathological) enunciations.

9 On the scatological implications of early modernist poetic glossolalia, see Annette Michelson, "De Stijl, Its Other Face: Abstraction and Cacophony, or What Was the Matter with Hegel?" *October* 22 (Fall 1982).

10 On the excremental symbolism and Surrealist poetics, see Allen S. Weiss, "Between the Sign of the Scorpion and the Sign of the Cross; *L'Age d'or,"* *Dada/Surrealism* 15 (1986); reprinted in Allen S. Weiss, *The Aesthetics of Excess.*

11 Jacques Derrida, "La Parole soufflée," in *Writing and Difference,* trans. Alan Bass (Chicago: University of Chicago Press, 1978), p. 181.

12 Guy Rosolato, "L'Expulsion," in *La Relation d'inconnu* (Paris: Gallimard, 1978), pp. 141–42.

13 Roland Barthes, "La musique, la voix, la langue," in *L'Obvie et l'obtus* (Paris: Seuil, 1982), p. 247.

14 The section on psychophonetics in this article is deeply indebted to Ivan Fónagy, *La vive voix: Essais de psycho-phonétique* (Paris: Payot, 1983) which provides an excellent synthesis and rich interpretation of current research.

15 Cited in Fónagy, *La vive voix,* p. 91.

16 See Fónagy, *La vive voix,* passim, for the empirical research on the relations between sound and meaning; this statistical research provides strong evidence for the nonarbitrary relation between signifier and signified.

17 Roman Jakobson, *Six Lectures on Sound and Meaning,* trans. John Mepham (Cambridge: MIT Press, 1978), p. 6.

18 Fónagy, *La vive voix,* p. 89.

19 Ibid., p. 112.

20 Elias Canetti, *Crowds and Power,* trans. Carol Stewart (New York: Continuum, 1981), p. 211.

21 Fónagy, *La vive voix,* p. 113.

22 Compare this text with the following passage from the opening pages of Witold Gombrowicz, *Ferdydurke,* trans. Eric Mosbacher (New York: Grove Press, 1968), pp. 12–14: "Half-asleep, I even imagined that my body was not entirely homogeneous, and that parts of it were not yet ma-

ture, that my head was laughing at and mocking my thigh, that my thigh was making merry at my head, that my finger was ridiculing my heart and my heart my brain, while my eye made sport of my nose and my nose of my eye, all to the accompaniment of loud bursts of crazy laughter – my limbs and the various parts of my body violently ridiculing each other in a general atmosphere of caustic and wounding raillery."

23 Friedrich Nietzsche, *Thus Spoke Zarathustra,* trans. Walter Kaufmann, in *The Portable Nietzsche.* (New York: Penguin, 1980), p. 146.

24 Ibid., pp. 249–50.

25 Cited in Mary Ann Doane, "Ideology and the Practice of Sound Editing and Mixing," in *The Cinematic Apparatus,* ed. Teresa De Lauretis and Stephen Heath (London: Macmillan, 1980), p. 54.

26 Ibid., p. 55. We should note that the development of stereophonic and quadraphonic recording and broadcasting was intended, for the most part, not to further the fragmentation of the senses but rather to unify them: the spatial differential play is unified by the temporal (melodic, narrative) aspects of the music, which performs a synthesizing function. In certain experimental works, such as those of Karlheinz Stockhausen, the multiplicity of sound channels is indeed foregrounded; but this is a studio or concert-hall effect much more than a radiophonic effect, given both the limitations of home two- or four-channel systems, and the usually less-than-ideal listening conditions in the average household.

27 One should consider Glenn Gould's seminal article, "The Prospects of Recording," in *The Glenn Gould Reader,* ed. Tim Page (New York: Vintage, 1990), for a discussion of the implications of both recording and playback technology for the future of music. He argues for the home listener's creative control by means of adjusting the sound of the stereophonic equipment, in striking parallel to Duchamp's infamous claim that it is the spectator who completes the work of art.

28 See Michel Chion, *La Voix au cinéma* (Paris: Editions de l'Etoile, 1982), pp. 25–33. These particular qualities of radiophonic reception permit the radio to function as a paranoid or poetic mechanism; for example, Varèse's *L'Astronome* begins with the reception of signals from the star Sirius; the protagonist in Jean Cocteau's *Orphée* (1950) receives poetic inspiration from incoherent messages transmitted through his car radio, a curious muse; Allen Ginsberg's paranoid mother hears spies on the radio, as recounted in his poem "Kaddish" (1959); and also in many cases of spiritualism, the medium receives transmissions of voices of the dead. Artaud was concerned about the problems of dubbing in the cinema – especially the incompatibilities between certain types of gesture and certain voices – as early as 1933, when he wrote "Les souffrances du 'dubbing'" (3:108–111).

29 Fónagy, *La vive voix,* pp. 209–10.

30 Two major theoretical issues are raised by the study of glossolalia in general and Artaud's recording in particular:

1. The investigation of glossolalia provides the test case for any structuralist, especially Saussurian, theory of the linguistic sign, necessitating a

revision of the notation of the arbitrary relation between signifier and signified, as well as of the idea of language as a pure system of differences. Jakobson shows how linguistic structures must be considered according to not only their differential but also (and especially) their distinctive features, which differ from language to language and even dialect to dialect; furthermore, as we have seen, the meanings of sounds are not completely arbitrary, but are in part corporeally and libidinally motivated.

2. The influence of Artaud on poststructuralist libido theory, especially Deleuze/Guattari in *Anti-Oedipus,* has yet to be fully studied. Suffice it to say for the moment that the notation of a "body without organs" originates in *Pour en finir avec le jugement de dieu* (13:104, 287). See Allen S. Weiss, *Perverse Desires and the Ambiguous Icon* (Albany: SUNY Press, 1994).

2. THE RADIO AS MUSICAL INSTRUMENT

1 John Harvith and Susan Edwards Harvith, eds. *Edison, Musicians, and the Phonograph: A Century in Retrospect* (Westport, Conn.: Greenwood Press, 1987), pp. 13–14.

2 Ibid., p. 10

3 Ibid., p. 185.

4 Ibid., p. 403.

5 Ibid., pp. 199–200.

6 Glenn Gould, "The Prospects of Recording" (1966), in *The Glenn Gould Reader* (New York: Vintage, 1990), p. 345.

7 Ibid., p. 352.

8 Ibid., p. 353. This belief would be instantiated in his numerous documentaries created in what he termed "contrapuntal radio," most notably *The Idea of North,* produced in 1967 for the Canadian Broadcasting Company, where he created a polyphony of human voices by means of splicing and overdubbing in the effort to establish radio as music.

9 Thomas Frost, cited in *Edison,* ed. Harvith and Harvith, p. 355.

10 Miha Pogacnik, cited in *Edison,* ed. Harvith and Harvith, p. 413.

11 Evan Eisenberg, *The Recording Angel: Explorations in Phonography* (New York: McGraw-Hill, 1987), p. 120.

12 Harry Smith, interview by John Cohen, *The Folk Song Magazine* 19, no. 1 (1969): 23.

13 Douglas Kahn, "Track Organology," *October,* no. 54 (1991): 78.

14 Ivan Fónagy, *La vive voix* (Paris: Payot, 1983), p. 118.

15 See Edgar Varèse, *Écrits* (Paris: Christian Bourgeois, 1983), pp. 53–54; Artaud, *Il n'y a plus de firmament,* in *Oeuvres complètes,* vol. 2, pp. 108–24 and the notes on pp. 335–37.

16 On modernist and experimental music, see Reginald Smith Brindle, *The New Music* (Oxford: Oxford University Press, 1975); Paul Griffiths, *Modern Music: The avant garde since 1945* (New York: Braziller, 1981); Michael Nyman, *Experimental Music: Cage and Beyond* (New York: Schirmer, 1981); H. H. Stuckenschmidt, *Twentieth Century Music* (New York: McGraw-Hill, 1979).

17 See Brindle, *New Music,* pp. 100–102; Stuckenschmidt, *Twentieth Century Music,* p. 177.

18 Michel Chion, *La musique électroacoustique* (Paris: P.U.F., 1982), p. 5.

19 Pierre Boulez, "Son et verbe" (1958), in *Relevés d'apprenti* (Paris: Le Seuil, 1966), p. 62. Note that this volume was edited by Paule Thévenin, who is also responsible for editing the complete works of Artaud.

20 Pierre Boulez, "Propositions" (1948), in *Relevés d'apprenti,* ed. Thévenin, p. 74.

21 For an excellent account of the Cage/Boulez debate, see Jonathan Scott Lee, "Par delà la *mimêsis:* Mallarmé, Boulez, et Cage," *Revue de l'esthétique,* nos. 13–14–15 (1988–89): 295–311. The locus classicus on the philosophical and musicological implications of Cage is Daniel Charles, *Gloses sur John Cage* (Paris: U.G.E., 10/18, 1978); see also Daniel Charles, "Interpenetration Without Obstruction: Senselessness Beyond Nonsense," *Public* 4/5 (1990), a special issue on "Sound" edited by Marc de Guerre and Janine Marchessault.

22 Pierre Boulez, "Alea," in *Relevés d'apprenti,* ed. Thévenin, pp. 41–55.

23 Ibid., p. 55.

24 Stéphane Mallarmé, "Variation sur un sujet," in *Oeuvres complètes* (Paris: Gallimard/Pléiade, 1945), p. 363.

25 Stéphane Mallarmé, "La musique et les lettres," in *Oeuvres complètes,* p. 644.

26 Mallarmé, "Variations," *Oeuvres complètes,* p. 366.

27 Ibid., p. 366.

28 Stéphane Mallarmé, "Un coup de dés," in *Oeuvres complètes,* pp. 453–77; Pierre Boulez, "Moment de Jean-Sébastien Bach," in *Relevés d'apprenti,* ed. Thévenin, p. 25.

29 Pierre Boulez and John Cage, *Correspondence* (Paris: Bourgois, 1991), p. 247. This letter is dated 5 September 1962, well after their break; it should be read in its entirety.

30 John Cage, interview by Daniel Charles, *For the Birds* (Boston: Marion Boyers, 1981), p. 222.

31 John Cage, "For More New Sounds," in *John Cage,* ed. Richard Kostelanetz (New York: RK Editions, 1970), p. 65.

32 See John Cage, "Cartridge Music," in *John Cage,* ed. Kostelanetz, pp. 144–45.

33 John Cage, "Experimental Music: Doctrine" (1955), in *Silence* (Middletown: Wesleyan University Press, 1961), p. 12.

34 Cited in Charles, *For the Birds,* pp. 181–82.

35 John Cage, "For More New Sounds," in *John Cage,* ed. Kostelanetz, p. 66.

36 John Cage, "Edgard Varèse," in *Silence,* p. 84.

37 See John Cage, "Williams Mix," in *John Cage,* ed. Kostelanetz, pp. 109–11.

38 On the influence of Duchamp and Cage on the New York art scene of the 1960s, see Calvin Tomkins, *The Bride and the Bachelors* (1965; reprint, New York: Penguin Books, 1981), and *Blam! The Explosion of Pop, Minimalism, and Performance, 1958–1964,* ed. Barbara Haskell (New York: The Whitney Museum and W. W. Norton, 1984).

39 John Cage, "26 Statements Re Duchamp," in *A Year from Monday* (1963; reprint, Middletown: Wesleyan University Press, 1975), pp. 70–72.

40 John Cage, *Empty Words* (Middletown: Wesleyan University Press, 1979), p. 65.

41 John Cage, "A Composer's Confessions" (1948), in *John Cage Writer,* ed. Richard Kostelanetz (New York: Limelight Editions, 1993), p. 43.

42 Alan Edward Beeby, *Sound Effects on Tape* (London: Tape Recording Magazine, 1966), p. 154; cited in R. Murray Schafer, *The Tuning of the World* (New York: Alfred A. Knopf, 1977), p. 49.

43 For the specific details of the compositional process, see John Cage, "To Describe the Process of Composition Used in *Music of Changes* and *Imaginary Landscape No. 4,"* in *Silence,* pp. 57–59.

44 Cited in Charles, *For the Birds,* p. 169.

45 Compare Cage's work, *WBAI* (1960): following Gordon Mumma's notion that designing electronic sound-producing circuits is a means of musical composing, *WBAI* (named for a New York City radio station famous for its countercultural activities in the 1960s and 1970s) is a score for the operation of machines.

46 Cited in Charles, *For the Birds,* p. 9.

3. MOUTHS OF DISQUIETUDE, LANGUAGE IN MUTATION

1 Denis Diderot, *Paradoxe sur le comédien* (1773; first published 1830; Paris: Gallimard/Pléiade, 1951), p. 1015.

2 Antonin Artaud, *Le théâtre et son double,* in *Oeuvres complètes* (Paris: Gallimard, 1964), vol. 4, p. 102. Subsequent references to Artaud's *Oeuvres complètes* will be cited in parentheses.

3 Diderot, *Paradoxe,* p. 1032.

4 Friedrich Nietzsche, "On Truth and Lie in an Extra-Moral Sense," in *The Portable Nietzsche,* trans. Walter Kaufmann (New York: Penguin, 1980), p. 46.

5 See Michel Thévoz, *Le langage de la rupture* (Paris: Presses Universitaires de France, 1978) and the special issue of *A+T* [*Art & Text*], no. 37 (1990) on Nonsense. Note that I have chosen to use the terms "mad," "insane," "mentally ill," "schizophrenic," "psychotic," "paranoid," according to the usage demanded by the varying contexts of my discussion, rather than make an ideological statement by choosing to use a single term throughout. Nevertheless, the history and ideologies determining such usages demand a thorough study, which is beyond the scope of this text. See Allen S. Weiss, *Shattered Forms: Art Brut, Phantasy, Modernism* (Albany: State University of New York Press, 1992).

6 Jean Dubuffet, "Un grand salut très différent au Martelandre," in *Écrits bruts,* ed. Michel Thévoz (Paris: Presses Universitares de France, 1979), p. 231.

7 Jean Dubuffet, "Gaston le zoologue," in *Prospectus et tous écrits suivants* (Paris: Gallimard, 1967), vol. 1, p. 325.

8 Roland Barthes, "Accordons la liberté de tracer" (1976), in *Le bruissement de la langue* (Paris: Le Seuil, 1984), p. 57.

9 Bernard Dupriez, *Gradus: Les procédés littéraires (Dictionnaire)* (Paris: Union Générale d'Editions, 1980), p. 465. These terms describe various modalities and styles of word jumbles, satirical farces, parodies, gibberish, nonsense, and amphigories.

10 The writings of Valère Novarina are all published in Paris by P.O.L., and consist of *Le drame de la vie* (1984); *Le discours aux animaux* (1987); *Théâtre* (1989) (the collected earlier theater works, including *L'Atelier volant, Le Babil des classes dangereuses, Le Monologue d'Adramélech, La lutte des morts, Falstafe*); *Le théâtre des paroles* (collected essays, 1989); *Vous qui habitez le temps* (1989); *Pendant la matière* (aphorisms, 1991); *Je suis* (1991); *L'Animal du temps* (1993); *L'Inquiétude* (1993); and *La Chair de l'homme* (1995). English translations, all by Allen S. Weiss, include: "Chaos," *Alea* 2 (1991); "During Matter" (selections) *A+T [Art & Text]*, no. 41 (1992); "Each Word Is a Drama," *A+T [Art & Text]*, no. 37 (1990); "Imperatives," *Sulfur* 27 (1990); "Theater of the Ears," *Discourse* 14, no. 2 (1992); *Letter to the Actors* and "Prolog" to *The Drama of Life* (*The Drama Review*, no. 138 (1993).

11 Valère Novarina, "Letter to the Actors," trans. Allen S. Weiss, *The Drama Review*, no. 138 (1993), p. 95. This letter was written in 1974 as a directive to the actors rehearsing his play *L'atelier volant;* it was published in Valère Novarina, *Le théâtre des paroles* (Paris: P.O.L., 1989).

12 Novarina, *Le discours aux animaux*, p. 321.

13 Valère Novarina, "Travailler pour l'incertain; aller sur la mer; passer sur une planche," interview by Philippe Di Meo, *L'Infini*, no. 19 (1987): 205.

14 Novarina, *Vous qui habitez le temps*, p. 19.

15 See Allen S. Weiss, "Radiophonic Art: The Voice of the Impossible Body," *Discourse* 14, no. 2 (1992).

16 Novarina, "Letter to the Actors," p. 11.

17 Ibid., p. 100.

18 Valère Novarina, "Le théâtre séparé," trans. Philippe Di Meo, *Furor*, no. 5 (1982): 87 (unpublished translation by Allen S. Weiss).

19 Michel Thévoz, *Le langage de la rupture* (Paris: Presses Univérsitaires de France, 1978), p. 79.

20 Jeanne Tripier, cited in Jean Dubuffet, "Messages et clichés de Jeanne Tripier la planétaire," in *L'Art Brut*, no. 8 (Paris: Compagnie de l'Art Brut, 1966), 23. See Allen S. Weiss, *Nostalgia for the Absolute: Obsession and Art Brut*, in the Los Angeles County Museum of Art catalog to the show *Parallel Visions* (1992), on the relations between Art Brut and Modern Art.

21 Tristan Tzara, *Oeuvres complètes* (Paris: Gallimard, 1975), p. 454. On sound poetry, see Henri Chopin, *Poésie sonore internationale* (Paris: Jean-Michel Place, 1979).

22 From Pierre Roy, *Cent comptines* (Paris: Henri Jonquières et Co., 1926), unpaginated.

23 Jean Dubuffet, *LER DLA CANPANE* [1948], in *Prospectus et tous Écrits suivants* (Paris: Gallimard, 1967), vol. 1, p. 119. Dubuffet's "Pièces littéraires" were published in vol. 1 of Dubuffet's *Prospectus. . . .* An excellent

reading of these works is that of Michel Thévoz, "Dubuffet le casseur de noix," in his *Détournement d'écriture* (Paris: Minuit, 1989).

24 Annette, cited in *Écrits bruts,* ed. Thévoz, pp. 43–44.

25 Samuel D., cited in *Écrits bruts,* ed. Thévoz, p. 63.

26 Samuel D., letter of 9 January 1954, cited in *Écrits bruts,* ed. Thévoz, p. 65.

27 Bobon and Thévoz are cited by André Blavier in *Les fous littéraires* (Paris: Éditions Henri Veyrier, 1982), pp. 114–15. This book is a vast compendium of works by what Blavier terms *les fous littéraires.*

28 Roman Jakobson, "Deux aspects du langage et deus types d'aphasie," in *Essais de linguistique générale*,* trans. Nicolas Ruwet (Paris: Minuit, 1963), pp. 43–67.

29 Octave Mannoni, "Writing and Madness," in *Psychosis and Sexual Identity,* pp. 44, 58. On Schreber, see *Psychosis and Sexual Identity: Toward a Post-Analytic View of the Schreber Case,* ed. David B. Allison, Prado de Oliveira, Mark Roberts, and Allen S. Weiss (Albany: State University of New York Press, 1988).

30 Friedrich Nietzsche, *Thus Spoke Zarathustra,* in *The Portable Nietzsche,* pp. 251–53.

31 Novarina, "Travailler pour l'incertain," p. 204.

4. LOST TONGUES AND DISARTICULATED VOICES

1 J. G. Ballard, Introduction to the French edition (1974) of *Crash* (1973; reprint, New York: Random House, 1985), p. 1.

2 J. G. Ballard, *Re/Search,* no. 8/9 (1984): 164.

3 Ballard, *Crash,* p. 13.

4 Gregory Whitehead, "The Forensic Theatre: Memory Plays for the Post-Mortem Condition," *Performing Arts Journal* 35/36 (1990): 99. It should be noted that this text includes an autobiographical account of Whitehead's near-fatal automobile crash and of the hospital stay in intensive care during which he believed that he had indeed lost his face.

5 Gilles Deleuze, *Francis Bacon: Logique de la sensation* (Paris: Éditions de la différence, 1981), vol. 1, p. 80.

6 Cited in Lex Wouterloot, "Silent Killing," *Mediamatic* 6, no. 4 (1992): 253.

7 For a detailed analysis of this work, in relation to Karen Bermann's *Theater of Operations* and David Wojnarowicz's "memoir of disintegration," see Thyrza Goodeve, "No Wound Ever Speaks for Itself," *Artforum* (January 1992).

8 See Jacques Attali, *Noise: The Political Economy of Music,* trans. Brain Massumi (Minneapolis: University of Minnesota Press, 1985), p. 91.

9 Ibid., p. 127; Attali's emphasis.

10 Gregory Whitehead, "Principia Schizophonica: On Noise, Gas, and the Broadcast Disembody," *A+T [Art & Text],* no. 37 (1990): 60.

11 Christof Migone, "Language is the flower of the mouth, with special guest the Radio Contortionist as flavour of the month," *Musicworks,* no. 53 (1992): 45, a special issue on "Radio-phonics" edited by Dan Lander.

12 Gregory Whitehead, "Who's There?: Notes on the Materiality of Radio," *A+T [Art & Text],* no. 31 (1989): 12.

13 Michel Chion, *La voix au cinéma* (Paris: Éditions de l'Étoile, 1982), pp. 25–33.

14 Whitehead, "Who's There?" p. 12.

15 Alberto Savinio, "Psyche," in *The Lives of the Gods,* trans. James Brook (London: Atlas, 1991), p. 8.

16 Whitehead, "Who's There?" p. 13.

17 Gregory Whitehead, "Holes in the Head: A Theatre for Radio Operations," *Performing Arts Journal,* no. 39 (1991): 90–91.

18 Whitehead, "The Forensic Theatre," p. 109.

19 Gregory Whitehead, "Radio Art Le Mômo: Gas Leaks, Shock Needles and Death Rattles," *Public,* no. 4/5 (1990): 141–49. The work of Douglas Kahn – coeditor with Gregory Whitehead of the first major anthology dealing with radio art, *Wireless Imagination: Sound, Radio, and the Avant-Garde* (Cambridge: MIT Press, 1992) – is apposite here. See Kahn's "A Better Parasite," *A+T* [*Art & Text*], no. 31 (1989); "Track Organology," *October,* no. 55 (1990); "Acoustic Sculpture, Deboned Voices," *Public,* no. 4/5 (1990–91); and his study of Whitehead's radio work *Dead Letters,* in *Performing Arts Journal* (1992).

20 William Burroughs, *The Ticket That Exploded* (New York: Grove Weidenfeld, 1987), pp. 50–51; Burrough's emphasis.

21 William Burroughs, "Electronic Revolution," interview by Daniel Odier, in *The Job* (New York: Penguin Books, 1989), pp. 174–203 passim.

22 Paul Virilio, "The Museum of Accidents," *Public,* no. 2 (1989): 81–85; first published in *Art Press,* no. 102 (1986): 13–14.

23 Cited in Rebecca Coyle, "Sound and Speed in Convocation," *Continuum* 6, no. 1 (1992): 131, a special issue on "Radio-Sound" edited by Toby Miller.

24 Gregory Whitehead, "Pressures of the Unspeakable: A Nervous System for the City of Sydney," *Continuum* 6, no. 1 (1992): 115.

25 Gregory Whitehead, *Pressures of the Unspeakable,* quote from unpublished text of the Australian Broadcasting Company project, which won the Prix Italia in 1992.

26 Whitehead, "Pressures," p. 116.

27 Guy Rosolato, "La voix: Entre corps et langage," in *La relation d'inconnu* (Paris: Gallimard, 1978), p. 39.

28 See Jacki Apple, "Screamers," *High Performance* (Spring 1992).

29 Attali, *Noise,* p. 91.

30 Pierre Fontanier, *Les figures du discours* (1821–30; reprint, Paris: Flammarion, 1977), p. 404.

31 This section of my text is indebted to Bernard Dupriez, *Gradus: Les procédés littéraires (Dictionnaire)* (Paris: Union Générale d'Editions, 1980), which in turn is based on numerous classic French rhetorical studies, notably Fontanier's *Les figures du discours.*

32 Paul Valéry, "Rhumbs," *Oeuvres complètes* (Paris: Gallimard/La Pléiade), vol. 2, p. 637.

33 Ivan Fónagy, *La vive voix: Essai de psycho-linguistique* (Paris: Payot, 1983), p. 267.

34 Cited in Roman Jakobson, "Linguistique et poétique," in *Essais de linguistique générale* (Paris: Minuit, 1963), vol. 1, p. 215.

35 Fónagy, *La vive voix,* p. 319.

36 Attali, *Noise,* p. 27.

37 Ibid., p. 33.

38 Ibid., p. 35.

POSTFACE

1 Villiers de l'Isle-Adam, "La machine à gloire," in *Contes cruels* (1874; reprint, Paris: Gallimard, 1983), p. 108.

2 Louis Wolfson, *Le Schizo et les langues* (Paris: Gallimard, 1970). On Wolfson, see Chantal Thomas, "The War Against the Mother Tongue," *A+T* [*Art & Text*], no. 37 (1990): 63–65; a fuller version of this section on Wolfson appeared in Allen S. Weiss, "Music and Madness," in *Shattered Forms: Art Brut, Phantasms, Modernism* (Albany: SUNY Press, 1992), pp. 89–102.

3 Wolfson, *Le Schizo,* p. 228.

4 Louis Wolfson, *Ma mère, musicienne, est morte de maladie maligne mardi à minuit au milieu du mois de mai mille977 au mouroir Memorial à Manhattan* (Paris: Navarin Éditeur, 1984), p. 11.

5 Ibid., p. 86.

6 Ibid., p. 109.

7 Ibid., p. 201.

8 The texts used in these productions are from Michel Thévoz, ed., *Écrits bruts* (Paris: Presses Universitaires de France, 1979); and John G. H. Oakes, ed., *In the Realms of the Unreal* (New York: Four Walls Eight Windows, 1991).

9 Christof Migone, "*Bruts* and *Bruits:* The Transpiring Transistor," *Sub Rosa* 2, no. 1 (1992): 3.

10 Ibid.

11 Christof Migone, "Language is the flower of the mouth, with special guest the Radio Contortionist as flavour of the month," *Musicworks,* no. 53 (1992): 47.

12 Ibid., p. 46.

SELECT BIBLIOGRAPHY

on Postwar Experimental Radio and Sound

Allison, David, John Hanhardt, Mark Roberts, and Allen S. Weiss, eds. *Nonsense.* Special issue of *A+T* [*Art & Text*], no. 37 (1990).

Antonin Artaud: Four Texts. Trans. and ed. Clayton Eshleman with Norman Glass. North Hollywood: Panjandrum Press, 1982.

Antonin Artaud: Selected Writings. Ed. Susan Sontag, trans. Helen Weaver. Berkeley: University of California Press, 1988.

Artaud, Antonin. *Pour en finir avec le jugement de dieu* (1948). In *Oeuvres complètes,* ed. Paul Thévenin (Paris: Gallimard, 1974), vol. 13. English translation by Clayton Eshleman in *Wire-*

less Imagination, ed. Douglas Kahn and Gregory Whitehead (Cambridge: MIT Press, 1992).

Artaud interdit, Artaud inédit. Special issue of *TXT,* no. 28 (1991).

Attali, Jacques. *Bruits: Essai sur l'économie politique de la musique.* Paris: Presses Universitaires de France, 1977.

Augaitis, Daina, and Dan Lander, eds. *Radio Rethink: Art, Sound, and Transmission.* Banff: Walter Phillips Gallery, 1994.

Barber, Stephen. *Antonin Artaud: Blows and Bombs.* Faber and Faber, 1993.

Blau, Herbert, ed. *Performance.* Special issue of *Discourse* 14, no. 2 (1992).

Book for the Unstable Media. 's-Hertogenbosch, Netherlands: V2 Organization, 1992.

Boulez, Pierre. *Par volonté et par hasard: Entretiens avec Célestin Deliège.* Paris: Editions du Seuil, 1975.

———. *Relevés d'apprenti.* Ed. Paul Thévenin. Paris: Le Seuil, 1966.

Boulez, Pierre, and John Cage, *Correspondence.* Paris: Bourgois, 1991.

Brindle, Reginald Smith. *The New Music.* Oxford: Oxford University Press, 1975.

Burroughs, William. Interview by Daniel Odier. In *The Job.* New York: Penguin, 1989.

———. *The Ticket That Exploded.* New York: Grove Weidenfeld, 1987.

Cage, John. *A Year From Monday.* Middletown: Wesleyan University Press, 1975.

———. *Empty Words.* Middletown: Wesleyan University Press, 1979.

———. *For the Birds.* John Cage in conversation with Daniel Charles. London: Marion Boyars, 1981.

———. *Je n'ai jamais écouté aucun son sans l'aimer: Le seul problème avec les sons, c'est la musique.* Trans. Daniel Charles. Paris: La main courante, La Souterraine, 1994.

———. *M: Writings '67–'72.* Middletown: Wesleyan University Press, 1974.

———. *Silence.* Middletown: Wesleyan University Press, 1961.

Charles, Daniel. *Gloses sur John Cage.* Paris: UGE, 1978.

Chion, Michel. *La musique électro-acoustique.* Paris: Presses Universitaires de France, 1982.

Chopin, Henri. *Poésie sonore internationale.* Paris: Jean-Michel Place, 1979.

Conversations with Glenn Gould. Interviews with Jonathan Cott. New York: Little, Brown, 1984.

Conversing with Cage. Ed. Richard Kostelanetz. New York: Limelight Editions, 1993.

Corbett, John. *Extended Play: Sounding Off from John Cage to Dr. Funkenstein*. Durham: Duke University Press, 1994.

Côté corps, côté jargons. Special issue of *TXT*, no. 29/30 (1992).

Davies, Shaun, Annemarie Jonson, and Eddy Jokovich, eds. *Essays in Sound*. Darlinghurst, Australia: Contemporary Sound Arts, 1992.

de Guerre, Marc, and Janine Marchessault, eds. *Sound*. Special issue of *Public*, no. 4/5 (1990–1991).

Eisenberg, Evan. *The Recording Angel: Explorations in Phonography*. New York: McGraw-Hill, 1987.

Fónagy, Ivan. *La vive voix: Essais de psycho-phonétique*. Paris: Payot, 1983.

Frost, Everett C., ed. *Radio Drama*. Special issue of *Theater Journal*, vol. 43, no. 3 (1991).

Gadda, Carlo Emilio. *L'art d'écrire pour la radio*. Trans. Guillaume Monsaingeon. Paris: Les Belles Lettres, 1993.

The Glenn Gould Reader. Ed. Tim Page. New York: Vintage, 1990.

Griffiths, Paul. *Modern Music: The Avant Garde Since 1945*. New York: Braziller, 1981.

Harrison, Martin. Tony MacGregor, and Virginia Madsen, eds. *Sound*. Special issue of *A+T [Art & Text]*, no. 31 (1989).

John Cage. Ed. Richard Kostelanetz. New York: RK Editions, 1970.

John Cage. Special issue of *Musicworks*, no. 52 (1992), ed. Eric de Visscher.

John Cage. Special issue of *Revue de l'esthétique*, nos. 13–14–15 (1988–89), ed. Daniel Charles.

John Cage: Writer. Ed. Richard Kostelanetz, New York: Limelight Editions, 1993.

Kahn, Douglas, and Gregory Whitehead, eds. *Wireless Imagination: Sound, Radio, and the Avant Garde*. Cambridge: MIT Press, 1992.

Knapp, Bettina. *Antonin Artaud: Man of Vision*. New York: Avon, 1969.

Lander, Dan, ed. *Radio-phonics*. Special issue of *Musicworks*, no. 53. (1992).

Lander, Dan, and Micah Lexier, eds. *Sound by Artists*. Banff: Walter Phillips Gallery, 1990.

Maeder, Thomas. *Antonin Artaud*. Paris: Plon, 1978.

Mallozzi, Lou, ed. "Audio Art." Special issue of *P-form,* no. 33 (1994).

Miller, Toby, ed. *Radio-Sound: Continuum* 6, no. 1 (1992).

Novarina, Valère. *Le théâtre des paroles*. Paris: P.O.L., 1989. [A list of Novarina's publications is given in chap. 3, n. 8.]

Nyman, Michael. *Experimental Music: Cage and Beyond*. New York: Schirmer, 1981.

Oor=Era. Special issue of *Mediamatic,* 6, no. 4 (1992).

Sound Re Visited. Amsterdam: Void Editions, 1987.

Strauss, Neil, and Dave Mandl, eds. *Radiotext(e)*. Special issue of *Semiotexte,* no. 16 (1993).

Stuckenschmidt, H. H. *Twentieth Century Music*. New York: McGraw-Hill, 1979.

Thévenin, Paule. *Antonin Artaud, ce Désespéré qui vous parle*. Paris: Éditions du Seuil, 1993.

La voix, l'écoute. Special issue of *Traverses,* no. 20 (1980).

Weiss, Allen S., *The Aesthetics of Excess*. Albany: State University of New York Press, 1989.

———. *Perverse Desire and the Ambiguous Icon*. Albany: State University of New York Press, 1994.

———. *Shattered Forms: Art Brut, Phantasms, Modernism*. Albany: State University of New York Press, 1992.

———, ed. "Art Radio." Dossier in *Java,* no. 12 (1994).

———, ed. *Experimental Radio*. Special issue of *The Drama Review* (forthcoming 1996).

Wolfson, Louis. *Ma mère, musicienne, est morte* . . . Paris: Navarin, 1984.

———. *Le Schizo et les langues*. Paris: Gallimard, 1970.

SELECTED DISCOGRAPHY

Antonin Artaud's *Pour en finir avec le jugement de dieu* has been released in 1986 by La Manufacture and I.N.A. (L'Institut national de la communication audiovisuelle) and distributed by Harmonia Mundi.

Since John Cage's death, an enormous amount of his works have been released on CD. His most famous recording, *The Twenty-five-Year Retrospective Concert of the Music of John Cage*, recorded in New York at Town Hall on May 15, 1958, has just been rereleased by Wergo on CD (WER 6247-2). This three-record set includes versions of *Imaginary Landscape no. 1* and *William's Mix*.

Valère Novarina's *Le théâtre des oreilles* has been issued as a cassette by Artalect (A.105) in 1983. Three readings of his works by André Marcon have been released on CD by Tristram (Paris): *Le Discours aux animaux* (1987), *L'Animal du temps* (1988), and *L'Inquiétude* (1993).

Most of Gregory Whitehead's works have been issued privately on cassette. More recent releases on CD: *How to Pronounce "Prosthesis"* appears on the *Tellus* CD #25 (1991); "The William Burroughs Tape Worm Mutation" is on *Musicworks* CD #53 (1991); *Pressures of the Unspeakable* appears on the second *Radius* CD, entitled *Transmissions from Broadcast Artists*, published by the Nonsequitur Foundation (1992); *The Pleasure of Ruins*, published by Staalplaat, S.T. CD 059 (1993), consisting of thirteen short pieces (including *If a voice like, then what?*, *The Problem with Bodies*, *Principa Schizophonica*, *O Solo Mio*, and *Eva, can I stab bats in a cave?*); *Dead Letters* appears as S.T. CD 091 (1994); and *How to Squeeze a Living Language from a Dead White Head* (including *Shake, Rattle, Roll* and *Degenerates in Dreamland*) is published as a V2 CD (1995).

Christof Migone's *Hole in the head [a] Tête a trou* was privately published. Several of the pieces derived from *écrits bruts*, appearing on the former cassette, have been released in 1994 on the CD *Radio Rethink: Art, Sound, Transmission*, published by the Walter Phillips Gallery in Banff, Canada, to accompany the book of the same title.

INDEX

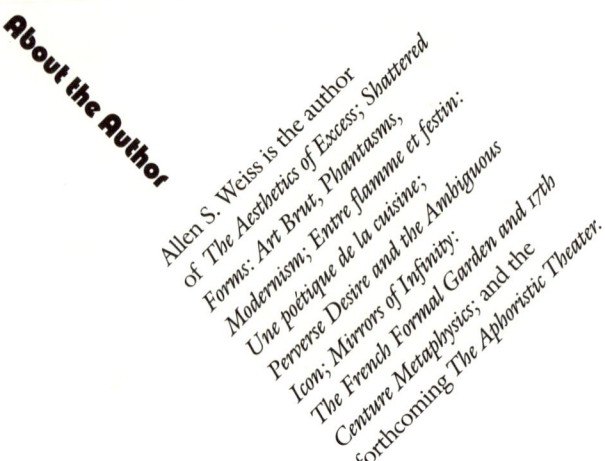

About the Author

Allen S. Weiss is the author
of *The Aesthetics of Excess; Shattered
Forms: Art Brut, Phantasms,
Modernism; Entre flamme et festin:
Une poétique de la cuisine;
Perverse Desire and the Ambiguous
Icon; Mirrors of Infinity:
The French Formal Garden and 17th
Century Metaphysics;* and the
forthcoming *The Aphoristic Theater.*

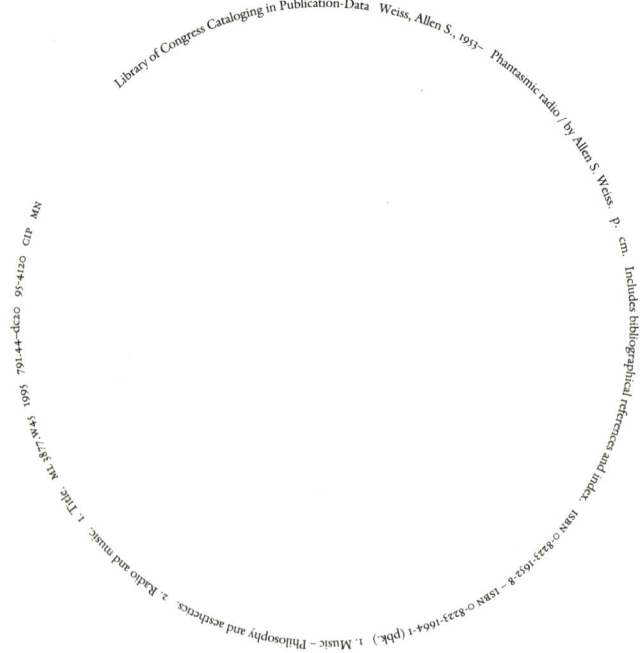

Library of Congress Cataloging in Publication-Data   Weiss, Allen S., 1953–   Phantasmic radio / by Allen S. Weiss.   p.   cm.   Includes bibliographical references and index   ISBN 0-8223-1652-8 - ISBN 0-8223-1664-1 (pbk.)   1. Music – Philosophy and aesthetics.   2. Radio and music.   I. Title.   ML3877.W45   1995   791.44–dc20   95-4120   CIP   MN